Connected
by
Nature's Law

ARI
Publishers

Michael Laitman, PhD

Connected—by Nature's Law

Copyright © 2013 by Michael Laitman

All rights reserved
Published by ARI Publishers
www.ariresearch.org   info@ariresearch.org
1057 Steeles Avenue West, Suite 532, Toronto, ON, M2R 3X1,
Canada
2009 85th Street #51, Brooklyn, New York, 11214, USA

Printed in Canada

No part of this book may be used or reproduced
in any manner without written permission of the publisher,
except in the case of brief quotations embodied
in critical articles or reviews.

ISBN: 978-1-897448-81-6
Library of Congress Control Number: 2013934488

Translation: Chaim Ratz
Associate Editor: Mary Miesem
Copy Editor: Claire Gerus
Layout: Baruch Khovov
Cover: Galina Kaplunovich, Inna Smirnova
Executive Editor: Benzion Girtz
Printing and Post Production: Uri Laitman

FIRST EDITION: JANUARY 2014
First printing

CONTENTS

FOREWORD

Our lives revolve around our connections and our relationships. In the end, our lives reflect our feelings toward each other. The changes in our lives lead us to understand the importance of our interconnections. The more we tap into that understanding and cultivate it, the more we will achieve mutual love.

By focusing on the connections between us, we can experience a new reality in a new world. In this way, we will actualize the good, peaceful, and balanced world that we desire.

We must be alert to what is happening between us. Inadvertently, we've often found ourselves tied in connections of self-centeredness and hatred, unable to tolerate each other even in our own families. Our current way of life is removing us from the reality of love and mutual consideration.

All our attempts to work out problems and crises using familiar tools have failed; now, we must acquire the know-how and the wisdom by which we can develop new sensations and new interconnections. Life is leading us to examine our connections and rebuild them. In a way, it is a rebirth into a new reality.

Connected—by Nature's Law will develop within us a new perspective from which we will try to resolve problems at a deeper level—one of interconnection with others. In resolving each problem, we will achieve love, concessions, and consideration between ourselves and others, just like a loving family.

If we open our eyes,

If we open our hearts,

We will feel how we are all connected

Because we, and the connections between us,

Are the most important things in life.

Modern-Day Slaves

For a person in 21st century society, work is the center of life. Society is what created that situation—so much so that even our free time, as far as vacations and social activities are concerned, are often initiated and managed by our workplaces. Some of these activities are organized by our workplaces to strengthen the connections between workers. These include such activities as trainings, fun days, trips, cultural events, and even family-supportive initiatives like daycare centers and summer camps. This is partly why workaholism has become such a prevalent addiction, especially among those in the middle class.

In the past, people didn't feel they were enslaved by their jobs. They felt much freer compared to our "modern-day slavery." Today the bulk of our time is spent at work, getting to it and returning from it. Work has become our primary activity, and one that takes over our lives.

When we meet someone, we immediately want to know his or her occupation, and we evaluate that person accordingly. We don't ask, "What do you like to do?" "What do you enjoy?" Instead, we ask, "What do you do for a living?" since work holds such a significant role in our lives. For this reason, a great concern for many of us is whether or not we will be fired, and if so, whether we will be able to find another job.

Today, our focus is almost entirely on our jobs. We're afraid of retirement, afraid that we won't know what to do with all that free time. We have no idea what it means to be free, nor have we any real desire to be so.

Even once we are at home after work, and even during vacations, we keep working, checking our emails and making calls to our work places. Modern communication helps us stay in touch with the system, keeping us captive to our working lives.

Over the last several decades, our approach to our lives has become such that we cannot see ourselves as free. "Free" should mean that we limit the time dedicated to work to three hours a day, during which we engage in what is necessary to maintain our society. In this way, we can provide for our society's needs after we have provided for our own. The rest of the time should be used for enjoying other things.

And yet, we cannot perceive this as possible. We think that if we don't work, we'll have nothing to do, yet nothing could be farther from the truth.

This mindset of work, work, work does not favor us as human beings. We are ruining and depleting Earth's resources, and we are immersed in this pattern much the way children become immersed in their games until an adult comes and pulls them away from it, saying, "Enough, you need to move on to other activities."

Alas, we cannot stop playing; we are addicted. The world and public opinion have "hooked" us on this game. Modern society has created a reality based on limited and purposeful connections, whose aim is to achieve very limited goals. Alongside this experience of limited connections, we have begun to feel a sense of meaninglessness in our lives. This is creating a crisis in every realm of our personal and social lives.

Today, we're at the threshold of a revolution. The gap between the environment we have created and Nature's imperatives is taking its toll. New conditions, both within us and in our environment, are pressing us with growing intensity, changing us from within and disintegrating the oppressive patterns of human society. Nature is pushing us to reach the next stage of our evolution as humans, to come to view life from a different perspective.

The reality in which work takes over most of our time is about to change. When that happens, people will not sit idly by, but will begin searching for another meaning to life. This is when we will truly learn what it means to "be human." As work hours shrink to the necessary minimum for sustenance, we will fill our lives with engagements appropriate to our level as human beings, engagements where we feel our souls.

This is a radical change that implies reorganization of the entire human society. This change is mandatory; we will have to go through this process due to pressures from within and without, or through awareness and initiative to immediately begin paving the way toward our new destination. Then, our perception of life will change, our economy will change, and industries will shrink and shift from over-production to producing solely what is needed to sustain us.

Work will become nothing more than a necessary tool for our survival, and our perception of the growing unemployment will change. Our free time will be channeled toward the primary purpose of our lives—to answer the question, "Why are we here in this life?" This question will arise in the majority of humanity, and will become the issue that directs our lives and all of our engagements.

Our goal now is to set up the infrastructure for an alternative environment that offers another avenue by which we will conduct our relationships. For example, in our future society, when I meet someone I won't ask about his or her job or profession (that person's "master"). It won't matter whether it's in hi-tech, banking, or mechanics. Instead, I'll be interested in what that person studies, his or her areas of interest, and the social circles to which he or she belongs.

In other words, I'll relate to the person in front of me as a human being, rather than as a slave indentured to a "master," a.k.a., a job. The job will lose its status as a person's ruler because people will engage only in what is essential to society.

To adapt to this future image, we need to imagine it and plan how we will shift from the current image into the projected one. We need to change from within, which is no simple task. It will entail revolutionizing our perceptions, sensations, and approaches to reality—a redesign of all our thought patterns. There is no greater revolution than this one.

Such a change affects the essence of life, the reason why we get up in the morning and go to sleep at night, the thoughts that run through our heads during the day, our achievements, and how others relate to us. Even the structure of society will change accordingly, and of course, the education system will evolve into a radically different one.

While the nature of the change is still unknown to most of us, it is nonetheless our future. The small steps we initiate preparing for it, gradually moving toward it, will allow us to see the direction of the shift and understand and welcome the process that is bound to happen.

It is similar to a child walking into kindergarten for the first time. He doesn't know what he has entered. He doesn't know that it's a part of an entire education system that will accompany him through the rest of his childhood years. Similarly, we are not yet aware of the global system and the processes that are about to unfold.

Nature demands that we be in "equivalence of form," meaning "in balance." As Nature is circular, a complete and harmonious system in all its actions, so should human society be built—circular and synchronized in all its parts. We will all benefit from being part of a balanced state, and the right connections between us will grant us "Nature's blessing."

"Connecting properly" means applying an integral form to every realm of life, including education, culture, family life, our attitude toward Nature, and to every realm of life. This is the only way we can be saved from the blows about to hit us, whose threat we can already feel under the strain of the global crises in ecology, economy, family values, and society.

Instead, a whole new perspective will open to us, putting us on a course toward resolving the major crisis we are in today. After all, the crisis is only the contradiction between the way we are managing ourselves and the essence of Nature, which presents itself as integral at every level of our lives.

This reality of Nature has only been revealed in the last century. Prior to that, the crisis was not comprehensive, but appeared to be part of a gradual process in the development and thriving of human society. It is only lately that we've begun to notice that Nature is closing in on us, presenting itself as an integral network, and presenting our inability to connect to that network.

Humanity's drives have become opposite to those of Nature, and we now sense that contrast as a crisis. This is the essence of the problem. The solution is simple: we need to balance ourselves with Nature, align ourselves with it. This is the goal of the studies we are now offering. It's becoming clear to us that, despite our sophistication, Nature will win, and that understanding is growing ever clearer in view of the problems we're seeing in all the systems we have built, which we can now barely manage.

In the coming years, unemployment will spread throughout the world. The unemployed will know that chances of finding a job are slim, and detachment from the job market will lead to frustration and disillusionment with life.

Yet, this process will take place alongside a vast change about to happen, in which free time will become the most qualitative, and where the unemployed will learn the real "humanities"—that is, what it means to be a human being.

All of humanity will learn the new information that will help people move through the next stage of our evolution.

With the help of integral study materials, we will understand our situation, the state of the world, and the reasons for everything that is happening. Without that knowledge it is impossible to reach the human level. The difference between a human being and any other animal is that man has consciousness: we understand and *consciously and willingly partake* of life. We know where we live, how we're operated, and how we should operate. In the end, we will learn to act as part of an integral humanity because reality dictates it.

The frameworks of study will become the new frameworks for everyone for an unlimited amount of time. People will treat these frameworks as a job, but unlike our current feelings about work, we will find in these studies, like children, constant rejuvenation.

The integral laws will have a strong impact on our lives. For example, a business that will operate *without* aspiration to sustain us will be treated as an infection that must be removed. That is, the ecological system dictates that we keep only what is necessary. This is a new approach, unlike the present one that says, "I feel like doing something new because I think I can sell it." Instead, we will adopt the opposite approach by which the less we produce and the less we sell, the better. As a result, everything will change.

In the near future, there will be a steep incline in unemployment, food shortages, and other problems stemming from the ecological problems we've created. High unemployment will invoke riots, leading to the disintegration of government and then, to anarchy.

Governments will have no choice but to collaborate and divide the existing resources. They will have to implement an innovative global plan, similar to the one we are presenting here. Otherwise, human society will collapse altogether and a world war will ensue.

In the global division of resources, man's economic participation in society will take place only according to society's essential needs. People's schedules will be managed over the Internet so that they will work for three or so hours to satisfy for their basic needs, and dedicate the majority of their time, say five hours a day, to academic studies, which will count as work.

The future unemployed individual will not be considered an outcast, but will make a decent salary and will be rewarded for study time, to which he or she will dedicate the bulk of the time. This will assure the person's future contribution and investment in the development of human society.

Our time frames will not change compared to what we've been accustomed to, but the content of our time, as well as the type of work we perform, will change. There will no longer be so much emphasis on work, such as when people thought about how to profit and succeed. Instead, the new framework will serve us as "gentle support," making certain we are not thrown out into the street, but can continue to make a decent living.

Every month, millions of people are losing their jobs with no substitutes in sight. They are often sent for needless trainings. But in the new framework of life, employment will not be offered to the unemployed, as is the case today. Instead, they will be offered a new approach to the world, one that paves our way to the next stage of our becoming human, becoming humane.

The problem is that today everyone wants to be a slave, except for a few tycoons who enjoy their fictitious freedom and free time. People feel that being preoccupied with something fills up their lives. Otherwise, with what will they fill them?

A person who seeks to be fulfilled searches for something to help realize his or her potential. It can be education, culture, or technology, but people want to be special, experts in something, to feel safe and secure. They believe that work will provide them with satisfaction and form a social environment for them. We are all searching for the same things.

Therefore, people will have many options from which they can develop in this new, integral living: communication, human relations, hi-tech, and anything that can be used to connect people into the system.

The integral system requires any profession that can help people train and adapt to this system. People can then become productive and creative with everything they learn and wish to do. Along with the new studies, a person immediately begins to ascend in his awareness, in the general perception.

This is why we need laws for mandatory education and mandatory occupation. Otherwise, in the future state, when 80% of the people have no work but will still have to be fed, they will destroy the remaining 20%.

The financial plights of the unemployed will not be limited to the unemployed, since food, heating, health care, and housing are necessities that must be given to all, not just to the unemployed. Otherwise, there will be mayhem. People are saving for their retirement, thinking they will be able to live in dignity once they retire, and sit comfortably in the Caribbean for the rest of their lives.

This isn't going to happen. They will barely be able to afford food and medication.

The world will not be able to provide for more than the necessities of life. The world needs to be organized in such a way that everyone has life's necessities. However, these will be provided only to those who join the new approach to work, assuming mandatory studies and meeting the needs of the community.

In short, in the new world, people who think only of themselves will not be able to cope. We have to consider the well-being of the entire community. This is Nature's Law, which is manifesting itself to us these days. Society must cultivate mutual concern wherein each person cares for everyone else as if they were parts of a single body, reciprocating with one another.

We are beginning to feel mutual concern, a mutual desire. These are the common life—the sensation of bonding among us, and the sensation of participation among us. With this perception we begin to feel timeless because we depart from our personal desires and begin to experience greater ones, those of the *collective*.

The world must be built from non-egoistic systems, and all the systems in the state must aim toward that goal— toward a single plan based on integrality and "mutual guarantee," which are necessary for today's society. If we refrain from doing so we will all fall prey to opportunism and destruction, and to an even greater contrast with

Nature. We need to make certain that we live like a family in a good neighborhood, in a good city, in a good country, in a good world.

Today we can study and grasp the process we are going through. This is wonderful. We are no longer blindly groping in the dark, and we are no longer fleeing the battlefield in every direction. We can unite, march ahead, and succeed in mitigating the processes we are going through.

"Integral education" deals with the structure of the new society and the new world from three aspects: the world, which is Nature; humanity within Nature; and the human being as part of humanity. Integral education also explains how we've arrived at the current state through the evolution of the ego, and how we should proceed henceforth toward a new common goal and common future.

CHAPTER ONE

A Crisis or Rebirth

ARE WE LIVING THE RESULTS OF OUR PAST MISTAKES?

Are we living the results of our past mistakes, or does life follow some comprehensive law, a general tendency? Or is it an inevitable process that we must experience, and only afterward obtain the benefits?

In truth, the term "crisis" is not a negative one. Although this is how we define the current situations—an economic crisis, a crisis in education, or a crisis in science—they are all aspects of a single, global and integral crisis, a crisis in every realm of human engagement. We use the term "crisis" to denote a problem, when in fact the meaning of the word is actually "birth into a new state," in this case, a state of being.

We know from experience that we tend to feel complacent and remain in a position with which we are familiar. It is hard for us to leave a job or decide on anything new in life. Habit sets the tone, and habits—as we all know—die hard, especially bad ones. Once a system is in place and we need not spend much energy to maintain it, we become quite lazy, leaning toward what is safe and familiar.

Yet, if we see a happy future destined for us, we march toward it with confidence and the transition becomes easy. If, however, the transition is difficult and forbidding, and we do not see the future, our situation will truly seem tragic.

Therefore, first we must examine whether or not our situation is indeed tragic. Think of a fetus growing in its mother's womb. It is lying in its protected shelter when a very unpleasant process begins to unfold—birth! Both mother and fetus experience great stress and accumulating pressure to the point that they cannot bear each other and the fetus must come out. Translated into our emotions, it is as though the fetus hates being inside its mother, while she appears to neither want to, nor be able to keep it inside any longer.

Then, by mutual rejection, birth occurs, and a baby is born into a bright, and beautiful world, greeted as one who has been rewarded with a new life on a new level. Where there were once a few ounces of flesh growing within another organism, a human has now emerged. It is still small, incapable of perceiving its surroundings, but it is the start of a new life.

This is very similar to the process that we, as a society, are going through. This is why our situation is like labor pangs before we emerge into a brand new world.

Previously, crises were not so radical that they were defined as "birth." We defined them as "steps in our evolution." There were many such steps in the history of humankind, but the current crisis is fundamentally different from those of the past.

We've always wanted to discover the new, forthcoming state (once we realized that some form of revolution in our lives was mandatory). It could be a social revolution, a political one, a technological revolution, or a revolution that arose because of some new discovery, such as new continents, new weapons, or a new technology such as the Internet, which helped us develop new connections.

Yet, until today, there has never been a revolution that so radically changed every aspect of our lives and the whole of humanity, affecting every continent, country, family, and person.

While we are still in the "prenatal" stage of the process, we cannot confidently say that this is what is happening. However, we can already see that we're heading toward birth. The situation, which we will define as our "prenatal crisis," increasingly presses on us, both collectively and individually. This is why we are increasingly unable to maintain family ties, increasingly reluctant to marry, and if we do, we are increasingly quick to divorce. We don't know how to raise our children, we cannot seem to cope in our jobs or in our social ties, and generally, we're being dragged into disorientation and disorder.

The reason we are defining the new state as a "full-blown revolution" or a "birth" of all humanity—and not the birth of a certain country or society—is that this state is manifesting all over the world. It is showing us how much we are all connected and affect one another. This is a global state, occurring simultaneously in every country and in each person. Indeed, this is an unprecedented situation.

21

But most important, we cannot see where this situation is leading us.

Throughout history, we've always advanced toward more developed societies, replacing one for another. Indeed, these changes happened through revolutions and wars over religion, resources, and territories. Even then, we've always felt we were headed toward a new and better state of being.

But while in the past one part of society agreed and welcomed the new situation and another part did not, or one country sensed the change and another did not, today no one has any clue as to the nature of the state that is forming. This has never happened to humanity until now.

Throughout the world, a global eco-shift is taking shape. Previous climate changes induced great changes in humanity, changes that prompted revolutions. The Ice Age, for instance, forced the Northern peoples to migrate southward, or to move from Siberia and Asia closer to Europe.

Other changes resulted from technological advances or from resistance to a certain government. But now, the changes are all happening *simultaneously*, through ecology and through man's nature. We can no longer cope even with such necessities as the continuation of the next generation, or such necessary systems as food provision, heating, family, and education. We have become dysfunctional. And most important, we cannot see the future toward which we are heading.

Can we see into the future? Is it possible to approach it with reason and understanding, as humans? A wise person looks ahead, examines, and tries to calculate. By doing so, one makes one's way easier and quicker, instead of groping in the dark as though one is blind. Especially now that the proportions are global, the thought of erring is alarming.

Information about the new, connected world will open our eyes to see reality from a new perspective. Primarily, it will present us with humanity's future state and reveal how best to arrive at it.

To make the transition pleasant and smooth, we must know the nature of the changes we will have to undergo, why specifically those changes must occur, the reasons for our current failures in our handling of reality, and the means by which to move into the new state.

Can we truly relate to our current state as a prenatal crisis, with Nature being our "midwife," with pressure from both our human nature and that of Nature itself pressing us and compelling us to change and arrive at the new state? Is this process natural for human development? If we knew the answers to these questions, could we predict what state would evolve ahead of time?

People who lived during the era of slavery didn't know that their next state would be one of relative freedom. They thought that slavery was the most convenient state. They had no desire to think independently, and were willing to work in return for food and lodging.

This was all they needed. The landlord tended to the slaves in order to profit from their work, and he provided them with shelter, food, and healthcare because he got from the slaves more than he invested in them. In this way, both parties benefited.

But slave owners discovered they would profit more if they let the slaves go free because their output was insufficient to justify keeping them on the premises. If the owners gave them freedom, the slaves would still work, the owners would still get their share, and it would be more profitable for them than to keep the slaves and tend to them. This was how society evolved to its next phase.

Today, as then, we are developing into a new state. Yet, why can't we see it? Why can't we plan it? There are intelligent people aplenty and there is vast experience from history and from science, so why are we groping about as if we were blind and incompetent? We can see the bewilderment at all the international conferences, every research institute, and every university. Sociologists, psychologists, and economists all seem to be lacking the ability to discover the solution to the crisis.

We know that something must change, perhaps everything must change, yet we don't know where to start. We have neither a means nor an end. We are indeed helpless.

Social development drives political development, as well as developments in every other realm of life—family, economy, education, culture, science, and technology. Today's social life began to develop eons ago, when we first realized that we couldn't provide for all our needs by ourselves.

Although we emerged from the animal kingdom, humans do not live in packs or flocks the way other animals do. It is inherent within us to seek to thrive, evolve, develop our environment, learn what life is about, and discover how we can improve our state of being. It is an egoistic drive. Everyone wants a better, safer, more peaceful life.

We also want to be superior to others. We are envious, and we seek power, respect, and lust. Indeed, these qualities motivated our development and progress, which is why man must lead a social life.

While we could cope in the woods if we tried, we would evolve as animals. There are cases where people were lost in the woods and lived there, growing up as animals. Under such conditions, a person acquires the form of an animal, losing the human within to such an extent that it becomes impossible to restore that person's social skills and reintegrate him into the human society. Thus, throughout the generations, our overriding thrust has been to develop society and our social environment.

As we evolve, we see that man does not evolve alone. Rather, everything depends on society. We develop the society, and through society our own lives develop. Both are interdependent.

You might say that today, each of us depends on thousands of people around the world. There is not a country in the world that doesn't provide for our needs, from food, clothing, building materials, heating and cooling, to everything else that we have and own. If not directly, then the provision is done through other countries—one country providing the raw materials and another providing the machines that manufacture the final product.

The more the world becomes differentiated into expertise, the more each of us has his or her job. Yet, that job is connected and synchronized with the rest of the people in the world. This way, we can provide myriad products beyond the basic food and clothing with which we sufficed in the past.

As we have evolved, we have increased our abilities to manufacture food and clothing. Afterwards, we developed means of transportation and other technologies, resulting in developing unique expertise, such as in economics, agriculture, machinery, arts and culture, and so forth.

Today, there are entire industries that develop products we don't need, such as sports or tourism, yet we feel we can't live without them. Thus, a famous musician may earn in an hour's performance what a blue-collar worker earns in a year or even more. We appreciate and even venerate things that are not necessary for our sustenance, but have become an absolute necessity to us.

If we calculate what we do every day to provide for our basic needs, compared to everything else we produce, we will see that 90% of what we produce is actually unnecessary for our survival. Yet, we need all these other things because without them, we'd feel that our lives weren't worth living, since these things belong to the human level of existence.

Thus, clearly, we inevitably depend on society. While we could live in caves if we had no other choice, our evolution as humans compels us to wish for more.

Today we are at a stage where detaching a person from society means sentencing that person to a sorrowful life. Such a person may be able to provide for life's necessities, enough to avoid starving, but for everything else, he or she would need other people. We need to produce everything that society needs, and then we will receive what we want from society. This is why our dependence on society is a given.

Indeed, what have we done wrong? How did we end up in a situation where we do not know how to handle ourselves? We are experiencing crises in society and in our own lives because we are currently feeling only the negative side of the crisis, only the pangs and not the birth.

If we examine ourselves and our development as humans, we will see that our entire development stems from our desires, from constantly wanting more. We previously had small desires. We wanted to live in the countryside with a few cows, a few hens, and a piece of land. A man had a wife and children, he lived his life, and he knew that these comprised his life.

Then, greater desires awakened in us, prompting us to begin to trade for what we wanted. We sold our products in the market and bought other products in return. For example, a farmer would arrive at the city and see that there was a new kind of plow that could till the ground more efficiently. He worked harder or borrowed money to buy the machine, and thus was able to produce bigger crops. This was how we evolved and began to interconnect as our growing egos prompted us to develop.

Our entire history is based on such developments in human desires. We always want more because our desires are constantly growing. We progress by looking at others and envying them. One person is successful at a particular enterprise, while others achieve in different directions. We learn because we are motivated by envy, lust, pursuit of honor, and a desire to dominate. We want to absorb from others what will benefit us, and be as successful as they are because our egos do not want us to feel like losers.

The development of human desires has caused every shift and revolution in human history. It is this development that has launched wars by which territories and nations were conquered. Then came a time of land discoveries, resulting in new areas of development. As technology and commerce evolved, we learned to process things in new ways. Now, at last, we've reached the final frontier: space.

And yet, ultimately, progress and development have brought us to a dead end. It started to become evident in the 1960s, when environmentalists and sociologists began to warn that humanity is at a standstill in terms of being able to determine where we should focus our future development. The space program helped us forget about this for a while, but that program, too, came to a premature end.

We circled the earth and reached the moon, but then what? It didn't help us much. For all our hopes of finding extraterrestrial life, everything we found was lifeless—no plants, no animals, and certainly no humans.

Instead, we have arrived at some kind of emptiness. We have evolved to the point where we have nowhere else to go. We cannot see where else to develop. Our own nature and the Nature we see around us have stopped opening themselves to us.

Thinkers and scientists in various fields are warning that we have reached the end of human development; in fact, they have even written books about the end of human development.

The human ego inflated, we evolved, and we believed that our development was unlimited, that we would produce more means of communication, vehicles, and even our own personal jets! But in the end, one who consumes all those products remains with emptiness, discovering that these do not deliver the satisfaction they had promised.

All of our progress has been born from our inherent desires, which were growing ceaselessly. Yet, they've suddenly stopped growing. Instead, we feel decadent.

While previously a man wanted a big family with many wives and many children, today men settle for one wife and one or two children. Today, life has become so tough, complicated, and complex that in developed countries people stay with their parents until they're 30 or even 40 years old.

People go to work and spend their entire salaries on themselves. They don't feel they need a family. They feel free, enjoying themselves, while their mothers take care of them. When the parents retire, they live on a pension and Social Security, and their children help them out and feel happy doing so.

We have built a society that has evolved to the point that you can buy ready-made food that you need simply heat in a microwave oven, and the meal is ready within minutes. Each person has his or her own apartment, which he or she shares with no one else, and when we grow old we have Social Security, health insurance, and hospitals to take care of us. Many of us feel that working hard simply doesn't pay off.

Our egos have grown so big we cannot connect with others, make efforts for them, or tend to them so they will want to tend to us. We don't feel that we can connect to another person unless we have a common interest to help each other out.

Today's spouses conduct their relationships like partnerships. They both work, both partake in payments, and are equal. In the past, the man would be the provider and the woman would stay home with the kids.

Today they both leave home for work in the morning, drop the kids off at school where they are supposedly educated, and pick them up in the evening on their way home. Once at home, it is each to himself or herself. Adults share the same chores and duties, and there is no longer a distinction between the father and the mother.

It turns out that we've come to a state where the family has lost its structure and has become a partnership, and as in all partnerships, we must examine whether it's worthwhile to keep the partnership going or break it up. This is why there are so many divorces, or people who don't wish to enter such a partnership in the first place. The ego, which has grown, is telling us it is not in our best interest to get into a "family partnership."

The education our children receive is very different from the one we received. The generation gap is such that they are often completely detached from us, almost as if they were a different species. They get a different education, they have different interests, and we can hardly understand who they are, how they speak, what they do, and what they like. The connection between the generations has been broken.

This state causes such thoughts as, "Why do I need kids if they bring me no pleasure and treat me like a walking wallet? While I may enjoy them when they're little, when they become teenagers I'll lose contact with them."

In the previous generation we could wait ten to fifteen years until we had grandchildren, which we could pamper while they were little, and that gave us some pleasure. But today even that's gone because the kids don't want to marry and have kids, so we won't have grandkids after all. In such a state, who needs kids? Of course, we don't make these calculations consciously, yet they exist subconsciously and lead many of us to conclude that we'd be better off without children.

It is all a result of the developed egos. Demographically, we've grown very quickly, but now the line has flattened out. In fact, studies are showing that birth rates the world over are falling, and soon the number of children will begin to decline.

Today there are still a few civilizations, such as Arab countries, with hereditary and religious motivations to have more kids. But in most countries, that drive has eased, and instead of having ten children in a family, there are only two or three children in each.

Alongside the disintegration of the family unit and the loss of kinship, another interesting, completely new phenomenon is taking shape: our society is becoming *connected*. Beyond the realization that banks, industry, and manufacturers are all globally connected and trade raw materials and products with each other, we are becoming mutually dependent in culture and education. This is not about knowing through the media what is happening everywhere on the globe. Rather, it is that we are becoming *dependent* on one another.

If that dependence is the kind that exists in a good family, it gives one the confidence of a family. But if it is a negative dependence, it leads to divorce, or worse, to violence.

Even though we're growing more hateful of each other and repel each other on a global scale, how can we divorce each other when Nature has closed us in on this thin crust? We are, in fact, globally interdependent, and we can neither divorce nor escape from one another.

Moreover, each day we are becoming *more* interdependent. Previously, when we were far away from one another, if there were conflicts we would kill one another, at worst. But with the weapons that exist today, any conflict can lead to the destruction of the entire world. Now, everyone depends on everyone else for better or for worse.

This is a big problem because at the same time, our egos are becoming even more intolerant and uncompromising. Our ability to reason is muffled by our intensifying hatred for each other, and we often fear that together with the weapons, our envy, lust, pursuit of honors and domination, and ruthlessness, we might end up destroying our entire world.

We can see how Nature is leading us into inescapable interdependence, unlike being in a family where we can divorce one another.

What do we do? The only solution is reconciliation among all the "members of the family," among all countries. And this should not be done by force or pressure, but via a mutual commitment to strive to complement one another— all the people and all the nations in the world.

Out of that solution, on which our lives depend, we will rearrange our social lives and our relationships just as a family. We must see what each of us needs in order to complement the needs of others. We need to figure out which kind of education we should inculcate into adults and children, and into the next generation to make it easier for them to join a good world when they grow up, a world of softness and warmth. At the same time, we should see how we can keep people from inciting against others.

Many scientific studies have shown that the world has become "round," connected and interdependent, and that we cannot escape it. Actually, it turns out that not only is our mutual interdependence inescapable, but each day people and nations are moving toward even greater collaboration.

It's becoming clearer that isolationism runs against the process we've been undergoing from the beginning of human evolution to this day. Resisting Nature's laws never works. In this case, it's even dangerous for both the isolationist country and for the rest of the world.

If I know the laws of Nature but don't keep them, I immediately harm myself. Every technology and science strives to emulate Nature. We develop tools to discover what else Nature has in store so we may use it to our benefit. Thus, the better we know and employ the laws of Nature, especially those concerning society and social psychology, the more we will gain. Otherwise we will have to begin a divorce process, which will ultimately manifest in a world war.

It is important to understand what we mean when we say that if we properly keep the laws of Nature on the human, psychological level, we will succeed. These are laws that operate within us as human beings, including human psychology and the psychology of society and family. Psychology is about understanding human nature and human relationships.

The better we know human nature and how to conduct our relationships, the better we will be able to build a society where everyone is happy, and where everyone makes concessions for others.

True, everyone wants to be "king of the hill," but we can show that we gain more by treating others as equal, by helping and supporting each other. If we show this, people will welcome the mutual concessions, understanding that there is no other way in a system where all are interdependent. In this way we will establish a society where everyone is happy.

Of course, our egos will constantly prompt us to resist the change. The ego always wants to rule, but public opinion will help us fight this. We will see just how the social environment affects and educates a person, how it can keep our egos in check. Indeed, public opinion can keep us from letting our egos loose, thus harming society. And once we rein in our egos, we will see that there is a lot to gain by using the ego in a socially favorable manner, and how the ego even benefits from such social interaction.

Our view of society and its influence should be the dominant, compelling, deciding element here. We need to learn who is man, what is the environment, and to what extent they influence one another. These relationships are Nature's laws, and we are a part of Nature. We must learn to be our own analysts, and analysts of human society. That way we'll be able to understand interpersonal relations and how to conduct them successfully.

We need to learn who we are, why we evolve as we do, and whether or not we can resist this development. It seems as though Nature is driving us toward something new and better; we just need to understand why, and then go along with it.

We also need to understand why we cannot see the future picture. After all, we've always seen it and evolved through our drive to discover, to rise, to grow. Today, this isn't so. On the contrary, we are withering, despairing, and losing our desire for anything.

It seems that this state, too, is needed for the next level of development to arise. It means we need to leave the current state and rise to a completely different one.

The reason for our despair, fatigue, and helplessness is our unwillingness to maintain the current situation. But by studying it, we are seemingly leaving it, washing up, putting on new clothes, entering a new world, and losing contact with the old one, which we made dirty, and where we harmed ourselves and others.

If we examine what we can take from our present world into the ideal world, we will see that we cannot take anything from it—not the broken family unit, not our relationships with our children, not our friendships, and not our jobs, if we even have one. When we reflect on our lives, we realize they are truly in a desperate state.

We are in despair because we cannot see what we have here and now. We cannot see a solution that might arise from the state we are in. It is like that in every country: we are all living from moment to moment, and more and more people understand that this is how things are, that we were born and therefore live.

We are in a very special situation. Research is showing that we are moving away from the way things are currently happening toward a new level of existence. We are actually leaping into a new degree and being born into a new world.

It is a world of different rules, which Nature has already begun to introduce to us. These are the integral rules, the laws of mutual dependence, the "round" world, a world of equality and unity. These are laws by which we live as a healthy family.

But does it only *seem* to us that we are heading toward such a world? Are we only dreaming about it, or is this the state that actually awaits humanity—one that we are bound to reach, either willingly and consciously or by forces that will impel us? If this is the situation, it will certainly be worthwhile to study the laws of the integral world because then we will know how to shift to that state pleasantly and comfortably.

We have to study these laws because in our previous state of development, we evolved by Nature's push from behind, through new desires that Nature evoked within us. Today it isn't so. We are at a dead end. We have no new desires to pave our way for us, so we must study our next step by ourselves, to learn its purpose and determine how we can accomplish it.

When we open the gate to the new life, we will see what lies before us. We will also have to learn by which means we can arrive at this new life. Unlike the instinctive development we've had in all previous generations—shifting from state to state, from one social level to another, and then to different forms of society—now we must evolve consciously. This is why we must study Nature's laws. Then, along with realizing these laws by understanding them, and knowing ourselves and our human society, we will shift into the new state.

It is as though we were giving birth to ourselves. This time, we must rise up and look at ourselves, at our situation and at what we are going through, from above. In the past, we've always gone with the flow, taken the chances that came our way, revolted and revolutionized our governance and our society. Today we must raise our level of awareness above our own lives and see Earth and human society from a global perspective. Then, from that perspective, we must further evolve.

It is the first time that Nature has demanded that each of us clearly know who we are, the kind of world we live in, and the state toward which we are developing. It is the first time we are being demanded to be "human" in the sense that we know and comprehend the *essence* of life.

Therefore, we need to understand that our studies are intended to help us revolutionize our lives and to elevate them to a new level, to wholeness.

When we research the inanimate, plant, and animate nature, as well as man—who lives within this picture—we find laws. We advance according to these laws and we call them "Nature." We are part of Nature; we're not outside of it; we are the result of Nature's evolution.

Human psychology, the science of human behavior, is also part of Nature's laws. It is a science that evolved relatively recently, some 100 years ago, because only then did we begin to feel we could evolve in a unique manner—consciously. We began to examine where we were developing, who we were, how we related to others, and why.

Until about a century ago, we wrote books that described only *how* we behaved. But since then, we've begun to research *why* we behaved as we did. Psychology is the study of the laws that affect humankind. Thus, it is a very important field of research because it helps us understand who we are, who others are, and how we can build a happy life through our connections with others.

The laws of Nature on the inanimate level are called "physics," on the vegetative level, "botany," and on the animate level, "zoology." On the human level, Nature's laws are called "psychology."

Children develop from year to year because their nature is developing within them. Each year a child develops in understanding, awareness, behavior, and physically, psychologically, and mentally. This is Nature's "Law of Development."

We can define what a child needs to know at specific ages, and what his or her physical competence should be at each age. We know these things because we already know the Law of Development. We know the dynamic and the process, and we cannot act otherwise because our actions are rooted within us and evolve within us.

We are part of Nature. Within us is an "engine" that develops each of us individually throughout our lives, and all of us together throughout history. In retrospect, we can draw conclusions as to why we have evolved in a certain way and what motivated us.

One can compare this evolution to that of a child, in whom there are bits of data that constantly develop, or to an animal cub, whose development we can anticipate. Similarly, society also has laws of development. We call those laws "Sociology." *Everything* in our world is built by laws. We don't really understand them because these are all new sciences, but the more we learn, the more we see that society's laws are like any other law.

People develop both personally and socially. All of these developments stem from the data embedded within us. The laws direct how we will build society, as well as how we will build ourselves. As time affects those data, it develops us accordingly.

Give a child food and take care of him, and you will see how he or she develops from year to year. But it is not the food that develops the child. The food only allows the genes to develop, but it is the genes that turn the child into an adult.

When a newborn develops from a single cell into a child, it is not because the parents decided this should take place; nor is it chance. The parents know in advance that the cell will become a child, and that the child will eventually become an adult. Everything comes from an information gene—certain data that is present there. This data receives "food" from outside and develops. It all happens by laws, as does everything that happens in human society.

Nature is something that evolves and leads the inanimate, vegetative, animate, and man in its development. We are all evolving: first evolved Earth, then came plants, then animals, and finally humans. Evolution began with the "Big Bang," and it is continuing through a process of joining together. The joining of parts develops them and makes them more united in both quantity and quality.

First, there was the inanimate. Then evolved plants that developed and began to grow; there was life in them. Then evolution arrived at the animate level, which evolved even further, to the point where each animal evolved individually. And finally came Man.

The question is, "Is there consistency, a law behind this development?" The laws exist; we know it from the past. We may not understand them, but the laws still exist.

We look at Nature and learn how it develops us as components of itself. Who is Man? For all our knowledge, are we not part of Nature? We exist in some bubble we call "the universe," and we study where we are and try to discover which laws govern this bubble.

There is no end to Nature's wisdom; we are only scratching the surface, and that shallow surface is our science. And yet, we cannot find our way, which is why we must study more of Nature's laws. It is actually fortunate that our discomfort is pushing us to study Nature so we can improve our situation.

To summarize, think of Nature as a bubble or ball. We live inside this ball, and within it are absolute laws that rule us. When we study Nature, we become aware of some of these rules. This exploration is called "science." However, we have yet to discover the vast majority of reality.

Knowing the laws of Nature helps us, as a collective, build a better life. We have TV, Internet, washing machines, dryers, and other appliances. All of them are results of studies we have made over the years. Compared to a person living in some remote village, pumping out water from a well, cooking with fire, and hand-washing clothes, we do these things quickly and effortlessly. We have all these appliances at home and can do myriad other things that, while living in a village in past generations, we weren't able to do.

Thus, technological developments gave us free time to engage in all kinds of works, which are far from being necessities.. The question is, "If we have so progressed in life, why have we ended up with such a cruel and empty life to the point of depression, insecurity, and anxiety?" "What have we done with the free time that technology and social development have given us?" "Why, instead of the peace and quiet of a country life—as physically hard as it was— have we arrived at a different kind of jungle?" "Why have we wasted our time and energy on creating such a hard and confusing life?"

Perhaps we need to arrive at a completely different way of life. Perhaps we should abandon the urban jungle and return to the village. In today's village, we'll have everything we need to provide for our necessities, we will work two hours a day, and we will spend the rest of our time doing other things. Is it possible that we can revolutionize our lives this way?

Thus far, we've tried to give an overview of our history from the evolution of our desires to our current situation. The desires that have driven human development have now become global desires, closing in on us and making us dependent on one another. They have made us one family, but it's a family in a state of severe crisis, due to our alienation from each other. The crisis is clearly a crisis in the "human family." If we create a new order in this family, we will resolve this crisis. Therefore, we have no other choice but to discover how we might find mutual understanding on a global level.

CHAPTER TWO

From Blindly Groping to Conscious Development

WHAT SHOULD WE DO IN ORDER TO BE HAPPY?

History shows that our lives change from generation to generation. Previously, people lived in small towns and villages. They lived and worked in the same place and rarely traveled. Today people work in one place, live in another, and often travel on business or vacation. People also relocate far more often and aren't confined to spending their lives in one place. Everything has become dynamic and subject to change.

Anyone who began his life in the first half of the previous century and now lives in the 21st century can see how the world has changed. Unlike all other parts of Nature—animals and plants—that hardly change for centuries, each human generation shows significant evolution in every realm.

This begs some questions: Why do we change from generation to generation? Is it not enough to be born and continue the species as before? What is the purpose of these changes, this development?

While we may not see the need for human development or its direction, we *can* observe *how* we grow. We see that a newborn baby has to grow in order to lead a good and fulfilling life as a grownup—to fulfill his or her wishes, change his or her life, have children and bequeath to them the possessions acquired throughout life. The children then continue the parents' life. In a sense, they are extensions of their parents' lives. But to achieve all that, a baby needs to grow and obtain the knowledge, strength, and perceptions that enable it to understand life and accomplish his or her goals.

Perhaps we, too, are like that. Perhaps we can compare those tens of thousands of years of evolution to the life of a single person, where each stage of evolution is like another stage in the child's growth.

We know how our own kids develop and how to provide them with what they need in order to develop, such as games and exercises. We then introduce them to a society that will develop them. But as to us, we ourselves don't know in what ways we are developing. This is why we don't notice the evolution of our desires, but consider their development incidental or random.

It's as though our evolving desires were happening by chance. One could compare it to parents regarding their child with wonder, asking, "Where did this child come from?" "Why?" "How do we rear it?" "What kind of education should we give him or her?" "Should he or she have company?" Should we enroll him or her in kindergarten?"

We seemingly don't know anything about our children. Indeed, how does a baby grow? It evolves by chance. The drives within them aren't enough to promote them toward the things they need as humans because the nature of our world is from the animate level. Therefore, we provide them with knowledge, sensations, exercise, music, education, and so forth. Put differently, we add to them the human level, the "speaking" level, enabling them to grow into the world we have created for them.

Conversely, while humanity is evolving from generation to generation, there is no one to make sure that it evolves correctly. Consequently, each new and more developed generation becomes more miserable, feeling more deficient and empty.

On the one hand, we want more technology and gadgets in our lives, but on the other hand, we feel so empty that today we're asking, "What have all of our developments given us? What have we achieved?"

Yes, we've reached outer space, sent spaceships to Mars, and landed on the moon, but no one is excited about these achievements anymore because we're taking them for granted. We can do almost anything on earth, but what about us? We don't know how to conduct ourselves in order to be happy. We're in a deep crisis, families are falling apart as divorce rates are soaring, children are suffering, parents are suffering, and society is suffering from terrorism and drugs. Where's our joy, our happiness?

Depression is the most common illness in the world. So if we think of humanity as a baby, it seems as if we don't have very good parents to take care of us and rear us properly.

If we examine Nature, we'll see that it has great concern for the correct development of each element. We, as parents, have great love for our children; we want to give them the best. We put our whole lives into it, developing for them all kinds of systems. Actually, the whole world works only to promote children, so they will have a better life.

But we are not succeeding, although Nature provides us with *all* the means to do so. Nature has given us love, without which we wouldn't pay attention to our children, but we love them instinctively, as animals love their offspring. In other words, Nature tends to the development of every single element and creature in a very special way. But while it prompts them to grow safely and well, for which Nature instills in parents instinctive love for their offspring and compels them to care for them, we humans are still failing to give them a good, secure life.

If we examine a fruit on a tree, we will see that initially it may appear unpleasant and not at all tasty. But as it grows and ripens, it becomes handsome, fragrant, and delicious.

Perhaps we are also like a fruit on a tree—going through similar forms of development that have yet to ripen. Perhaps we're like a green, hard, sour apple, which no one knows will grow into a beautiful fruit unless we know it from experience.

The same happens with humans. It takes at least 20 years before a child grows and becomes fit for life as a grownup, able to learn, implement knowledge, and "make one's mark in the world." Conversely, an animal needs only a few weeks or a few months to develop. However, it doesn't advance as much and remains an animal, knowing only how to take care of its needs instinctively. It doesn't change itself or the world.

Therefore, we can conclude that our development is gradual, like that of a fruit that is foul-tasting in its inception, but finally grows sweet and tasty. And the longer and more stages it requires to develop, the more complex will be its final development and the greater its achievements.

From all that we learn from Nature, we can conclude that we are now going through a very special development: From generation to generation, we are evolving as a single creature still in its early stages of development. This is why we seem so "sour" and unsuccessful. However, at the conclusion of our development we are guaranteed to be "sweet" and wholesome.

Of the four levels of reality—still (inanimate), vegetative, animate, and human—the human species is at the top. Man is the apex of creation. This is why his development is the longest, and the stages he goes through—from the beginning of his development to the end—are so extreme that the final version seems like a completely different species from the original one. If we consider the direction Nature is taking us we will be able to draw the right conclusion about ourselves and Nature's "attitude" toward us, but only if we can see, from the beginning, how it will end.

If we saw the apple in its early stages of development, we'd think that it would be completely useless. Only in the end do we see Nature's great wisdom in developing it into such a beautiful and delicious fruit.

Following the Law of Development, we, too, are under the same pattern of development, and the purpose of our development is undoubtedly to bring us to a good, wholesome, sweet, and perfect state.

Now, what might the perfect state be? If Nature gradually develops us so that in each generation we acquire more sensations and more perceptions, acquire more and more of the nature of Creation, rise above it, and become able to absorb and govern it, then our final development will truly achieve the highest degree of reality.

So how *do* we evolve, through what? What are the forces that develop us? Well, development can be similar to that of a child evolving through its natural drives. In the absence of external, human stimuli, a child will grow like an animal, not knowing how to do things that humanity has devised for it. If we don't put a child in the company of other children, it won't know how to be in the company of humans, how to play with them, how to connect with them, how to help them, and how to be helped by them.

But if we build around that child a society such as kindergarten, school, educators, games, and parents who constantly try to promote it, we can significantly accelerate its development. That promotion should not be through natural drives, but through stimuli from the environment that pull it forward toward development. We can teach children music, painting, sculpturing, dancing, computers, and so on, and then their development is through these means rather than through natural ones.

Thus, there are two forces of development. One way of developing is through a force that pushes from behind. This is the Force of Nature. The other is a force that pulls from before. A child is affected by that force, if he or she is in the right environment.

The same principle applies to us. If we understand that we develop like the fruit on the tree—from bad states to good ones—then perhaps by building ourselves an environment that will pull us forward we will quickly and pleasantly evolve through our stages of development. We will not have to be pushed from behind by blows and suffering. Instead, we will develop through favorable means such as games, explanations, and other pleasant influences.

Today we're in such a tragic situation, a comprehensive crisis that humanity doesn't know what to do about it. We are like babies standing in the middle of the room feeling lost and abandoned, without knowing what to do or where to turn for help.

With crises in families, in education, in culture, in spousal relationships, parent-child relationships, drugs, divorces, science, and especially the economic and ecological crises, we can't see anything to look forward to. For all we know, in two weeks there could be a hurricane that would leave us without power and inundated in water. We just don't know what to expect anymore.

In such a state, how can we build our lives so we can develop as nicely and quickly as possible? Our development depends on the environment, and we can build it in such a way that it develops us more quickly. It took us thousands of years of development to be able to offer children games, computers, music, dancing, swimming, sports, and so forth. We now understand that it's good if we give them these things, so perhaps we should also do the same for adults.

If we want to develop something more quickly, we need to build an "apparatus" that accelerates the development.

Think of an incubator for eggs. We don't wait until they hatch. Instead, we put them in an incubator and get lots of healthy chicks without having to wait for the chicken to produce the same results.

In other words, we can provide ourselves with correct, fast development, avoid all kinds of blows along the way, and develop well, like a child in a family that can give it the right things at the right time. Thus, the child will not experience any problems as it grows and our problem will only be to understand how we can best develop.

Here's where we arrive at the solution. The current crisis is a global and integral one. This means that on the one hand, a crisis, a plight, is forming throughout the world. At the same time, this forbidding situation is actually a demonstration of our lack of development.

Today our studies show that we are totally interdependent, and our inability to interconnect is the source of all our troubles. This inability makes our lives miserable, unsafe, and frightening. Something is stopping us from bonding correctly, although by bonding we would eliminate the majority of our problems.

We can also see it in the process of development we've gone through. From generation to generation humanity increased its integration, cooperation, and interdependence in education and culture, industry, and so forth. Now we have come to a state where we're not only dependent on each other for our livelihoods, we are dependent on each other in a *human* way. At the same time, we've come to a point where we cannot connect to one another, and that disconnect among us prevents us from establishing a better and safer life.

In a sense, we're like a family living under the same roof, yet we cannot get along. However, unlike a family, we cannot divorce because we have no other Earth to colonize.

Studies published on this topic show that the desirable way for us to develop is by bonding, by being connected like lovebirds. If all of humanity arrived at a state of comprehensive connectedness, we would all be happy. This makes what we must do quite clear: we must build an environment that will teach us how to connect properly.

In trying to establish for ourselves the proper environment we are like wise children who understand that they must grow up well and correctly, and therefore set up an appropriate environment for themselves. These wise ones go to the neighbors and say, "We'll pay you to act out what it's like to be connected, and thus draw all of us into that bonding. We know that if the other children see such examples they will grow up correctly, so we want to save ourselves from our situation through your example."

Another example: If I want to be a musician, but I don't have a strong enough desire to study music, I must have someone stimulating me, convincing me that music is beautiful, great, special. So I may pay some musicians to come by and play for me, constantly talk about music, let me be around their instruments, compose something in my presence, and thus impress me. This will give me the profound impression that music is a great thing, that their collaboration and the harmony in their music are very significant and important. As I watch them, I thus build an environment through which I can develop.

It doesn't matter if I pay them; what counts is the result. It's like being on a sports team and being impressed by the other players. The most important thing for us is the society.

We can create that society by ourselves, but it is best if it is created for us by people who know how to do it. There are many intelligent people, including scientists who understand human development, and we just need to follow their suggestions. They say that we should build an environment that will affect all of us, and by which we will progress in positive directions in a favorable, gradual manner. Then we will be like a fruit that ripens before difficulties arise and force us to grow from blows. We will run ahead in our development, just like an egg developed in an incubator.

If we examine man's development over millennia, we will see that our current situation is not good. And yet, we know how we can pull ourselves out of the predicament, rather than wait for whatever happens. Instead of waiting we can listen to those who say that we need a good environment in which to develop, that will bring us to the perfect state of development stage by stage, favorably, easily, and gently.

Thus, all we need is a good environment. With a good environment, I begin to feel what is bad in my own nature—that I'm an egoist, that I don't want to bond, that I'm lazy, uncaring, and indifferent. There are many qualities in me that I don't want to develop. But precisely through recognizing the bad within me I understand that we must create a better society.

And yet, we don't need to develop just any environment. We need to create one that takes care of each and every one of us, so no one remains idle and "out of the game." Just as kids grow smarter and stronger by playing games, we will achieve our perfect form and have a good life through our own games in a society that promotes us.

In that state, the environment will reflect the opposite of today's crises. There will be no divorces, and people will be on good terms with each other. Children will get along with their parents, international relations will be smooth, there will be no wars, no weapons, no terrorism, no drugs, and no debts. We must build such a role-model society so it can influence us. We need its values so it will persuade us, or "re-program" us, into becoming similar to it.

Now, we are embarking on a path that forces us to develop ourselves. Thus far, we've been evolving through Nature's "pushing" force, and we were unable to control the pace or the way in which we developed. Now both the pace and the method depend on us. They depend on our awareness, on the extent to which we understand what we should be like in the future. Then we must aim ourselves toward this objective.

The crisis is global. We've stopped developing and will remain in a standstill until we understand that in each of the next stages of our development we must first be aware of the stage and then cultivate a desire for it. In other words, henceforth our growth will no longer be instinctive. Instead, it will occur by increasing our awareness at each stage.

This is the meaning of "being at the human stage of development," the "speaking" degree. Something new is evolving, an understanding of Nature, our new goal, and our need to comprehend and integrate parts of Nature's system into our evolution.

In this last stage of humanity's development, the "fruit," meaning us, must acquire the sweetness, color, and fragrance of ripeness. All those qualities come from the fruit itself, according to Nature's love for it. Nature develops us just as a mother cares for her child. We must achieve that same force of love, bestowal, and mutuality. We must achieve global connectedness among us and with Nature.

Such connectedness happens only by awareness— when we understand and feel this development—and how we experience it. We cannot guarantee a good life for people without their first raising their levels of perception and sensation. They must acquire awareness; they must know what kind of world they live in, and discover the *whole* of Nature.

Humanity will not advance without each person becoming wise, knowing why he or she was born, understanding the nature that's promoting us, and for what purpose. Otherwise, we will only suffer blows.

To summarize, Nature is admitting us into the perfect state in stages. Thus far, we have advanced through a compelling force. But from now on, we can advance only by becoming aware of how we develop. We can improve, sweeten, and rush our development from now on using the environment, just as we have done in every other realm thus far.

Children develop through the environment; grownups develop through the environment; everything changes through the environment. Take AA groups, for example, or rehabilitation centers, or weight-watching groups. Just like them, we should build up the influence of the environment on people, and then we will develop like good kids who grow up in a good environment. In addition, we will build a good environment for our children so they, too, will grow up to be happy, wholesome individuals.

Parents would love to bring their kids to a place where warmth and good relationships help them connect with each other, and encourage them to be open and trust one another without fear of violence or cruelty. There is nothing like this in our world—a place that allows you to develop gently.

In such an environment, children would grow up with the ability to absorb information and become perceptive. They would develop immense capabilities. They wouldn't feel they had to constantly protect themselves in a hostile environment.

We adults don't understand what it means to live in a positive environment. It can be compared to being a baby in its mother's arms, not seeing or feeling anything but her comfort and security. Only this kind of feeling can give an infant the strength to develop. We don't have that feeling, and this is why we have stopped evolving.

On the one hand, a crisis can be a shattering. On the other hand, it is like being reborn. Thus, what do we need in order to be happy? We need a positive environment that brings us to a state of feeling good, safe, and confident. We need an environment where we feel that the whole world wants our best and cares for us. Then, we will care for others in a place that is warm and pleasant, a world of love.

CHAPTER THREE

Man as a Product of the Environment

TO WHAT EXTENT DO WE HAVE FREE CHOICE?

Humanity is in the midst of an evolutionary process, changing as it unfolds. Through our development from generation to generation over thousands of years, we've come to a very special situation: we now exist on the planet as a global, connected society. As we evolved, we have acquired knowledge, capabilities, and the power to obtain sensations and perceptions we did not previously possess.

We are still in the midst of the development and do not see its end, but we hope that soon we will experience a positive result. Therefore, let us try to see what is so special about our situation, and what we must do to ensure that we undergo a smooth transition into an enlightened state of confidence, prosperity, and good living.

As we evolve, we experience many different states that we cannot really control. We change our lives according to these states, and try to make them more convenient. We change society, family life, education, culture, and human relations. We try to make our lives as good and as comfortable as possible because at the very root of each of us is a desire to enjoy.

We evolve gradually using whatever means is at our disposal at each step. When we wish to change our lives, we evolve through science. We study Nature and try to learn from its examples so we can modify ourselves accordingly. We try to learn more about the laws of Nature in order to protect ourselves.

For example, we study climatology to understand the implications of each season and climate. We study our own bodies, too, so we can prepare medicines for our illnesses. We also study human nature, and accordingly develop home appliances to ease our tasks—washing machines, dryers, ovens, and so on. Thus, we strive to have as good and as comfortable an environment as possible. In this way we try to escape our minuscule personal sufferings, as well as the mammoth global suffering.

In addition, we try to advance toward a better life and make the best of every situation. It is human nature to strive for it, and we try to use every means to implement it.

We develop through drives that arise from within. Each moment, at each stage, a new desire evolves within each of us, and we follow that desire. If we examine ourselves, we will see that we are just like kids, wanting different things each moment. We want to eat, drink, perhaps look at something interesting, and sleep. Alas, most of us must work for a living.

We constantly develop under the influence of forces. For example, there is a force that pushes from behind, compellingly, such as to work or run some errands. Nothing comes easily for us; pleasures don't come to us and satisfy us as we want. In our future state, this will be possible, but we haven't yet discovered such fulfillment.

Where do our desires come from? Some of them come from our own physiology, from our body's needs to provide itself with food, rest, and fill the in-between with something interesting.

We divide our desires into food, sex, and family—basics without which we, as members of the animal kingdom, would not exist. Additionally, we need things that pertain to the human species, such as money, respect, power, knowledge, culture, education, religion, and many others that we develop, and that are as important to us as food, sex, and family.

We are, however, often willing to sacrifice much of our desire for food, sex, and family in favor of more education, culture, and science. There are people who are willing to make great sacrifices to obtain money, respect, or power. They care very little about food, sex, or family, and satisfy those needs only as necessary.

The desires for food, sex, family, money, respect, power, and knowledge exist in all of us in different measures, and each of us tries to realize them as best as possible. The extent to which one is willing to pursue certain desires, and the way one pursues them, depend on the environment and on one's education. The balance between the actualization of the natural tendencies on the physical level and the actualization of the tendencies on the human, "speaking" level also depends on the environment. This affects which tendencies we will develop more, and which we will develop less.

If we place a child in a certain environment, such as one that appreciates science, while the child is still "a blank slate," he or she will learn from the environment about the importance of science and how respectable it is to do well in it. While every person has some degree of desire for science, the environment can encourage that particular tendency. That is, the environment can change the balance within an individual's tendencies and develop some more than others.

If parents want their children to develop in a certain direction, they will place them in the appropriate environment, such as a sports team or a music school. Even if a child isn't fond of music, it will learn it, understand it, and appreciate it for the rest of his or her life.

So it is in everything. A child's development comes via its environment, and the parents' abilities to develop the child eventually determine the direction of his or her development, encouraging certain tendencies more than others, and even suppressing some desires. Thus, as we grow, our free choice becomes limited, designed by the environment into which we were born and raised as children. As adults, we will pursue that direction for the rest of our lives.

As to the question, "To what extent do we have free choice?" We do have a small amount of free choice, but in the end, even the little we have comes from the environment. We're affected by trends or friends who "happen" to be around us, instilling all kinds of values and preferences in us.

We have to understand that "recollections" from experiences we had in our previous lives also appear in us. These recollections are pieces of information from previous lives, or "incarnations," through which we develop. Thus, not only are we born into a more advanced society in each lifetime, but new tendencies also evolve within us in each generation due to those recollections through which we develop.

We feel it especially vividly today in our children, who are grasping new technologies much faster than we adults. It's as if they were born with preexisting preparations, scrutinies, and qualities that enable them to perceive the world and succeed in modern life. They quickly learn how to operate cell phones, computers, and other new technologies, while older persons do it with difficulty, if at all. It's as if this newer generation were born prepared to look at everything according to its inner nature. They approach those innovations and understand them as if they were Indigo Children, as though they landed from outer space into our world.

From all the above, we can conclude that within us are "recollections," information genes that evolve from generation to generation. We call them "incarnations." This is not mysticism. Rather, it's a description of a state in which we are all interconnected, as we are now discovering.

As there are physical force fields, such as electromagnetic fields or gravitational force fields, there is an all-embracing field of thought, a desire that connects us all beyond time and distance, and we are in that field. This is how we convey to one another the information we acquire from generation to generation. Our bodies, which are in this field, absorb the information, making the next generation prepared for life in the new state, the new era.

Our entire development is through the environment. Were it not for the environment, we wouldn't be developing, despite our recollections from previous lives.

Even our bodies are highly dependent on the society in which we develop. Man is very adaptable compared to animals. Cats or dogs, which have been with humans for millennia and have grown accustomed to man's company, still change very little. True, they cannot live like wild cats or dogs, and they already have a different nature, passing on to their offspring a different attitude toward man and toward the environment. However, they aren't as adaptable as humans. People who mingle in a certain environment and are impressed with it become used to it in a much more substantial manner.

Because we're all dependent on the environment, this is the first thing we should notice in education—the environment as a cause in one's development, since the whole of one's future depends on it. If we, as parents, change the social environment of our children, or even our own social environment, we thus change our natures, our desires, and our outlook on life. Therefore, we should carefully examine and think about where we go, with which friends, in what circles we spend our time, and to whom we "give ourselves up."

Therefore, we need to teach people about all kinds of circles, different environments in one's surroundings, and the extent to which one depends on them and can manage his or her life through them. If, through all these examples, we see that man is truly an offshoot of the environment, then it's very important for us to set up wholesome environments for all of humanity. They should be set up offering such variety that anyone will be able to fit into one environment or another, according to individual tendencies and character. This way, a person will be able to develop in the best way to become a complete human being. This is why in our education we must see to it that such societies are available for us all.

If we examine even more deeply, we will see that there are internal conditions within us, genes with which we were born, and various tendencies acquired through the first years of our lives when we are close to our mothers, and later on from the environment. This is why we need to have kindergartens, after-school classes for young children, and schools and after-school classes for older children. This ensures that each child truly has a choice of classes and social environments by which to realize his or her potential in every respect. We even need to see that children have the means to develop tendencies in which they might not excel, so they become internally rich individuals. Therefore, they should learn music, literature, theatre, and education.

A person also needs to have a family, raise children, to know how to relate to one's spouse and one's friends correctly, and how to handle oneself at work and in society as a whole. We must give people examples that will show them the right way to behave, using the right environment. Then they will be easygoing and will eventually thrive and succeed.

Two elements lead and direct us each moment in life: our natural tendencies and the main cause—the environment and its effects on those natural tendencies. Everything depends on the extent to which we are taught how to choose environments that will lead us toward more developed states in which we will acquire more confidence and comfort, and achieve the best possible level of existence. This is how we continually develop ourselves.

Thus, the way we can be certain that our children will have a better life than ours, that the next generation will be a better one, with a safer future, is by surrounding our children with an environment that designs and educates them. That environment will turn them into people who enhance their good inclinations and do not suppress those less favorable, but rather improve and enhance them.

Each of us possesses tendencies to act unfavorably toward others. Favorable or unfavorable actions are determined by our attitude toward ourselves and toward our environments. Concerning our attitude toward ourselves, we must teach people how to avoid harming ourselves, particularly physically, because although we naturally protect ourselves, we also possess self-destructive penchants.

We also need to set straight our attitude toward the environment, toward the inanimate, vegetative, and animate—the environment we live in and which we must maintain. We live inside of Nature. The inanimate, vegetative, and animate are imperative to us because we receive from them everything we have and need. We eat our food from Nature and we are dependent upon climate. This is why we must teach people how to preserve the ecology in their environment.

Additionally, we need to teach people how to relate to the human society. If we affect society favorably, that attitude ultimately reflects on us and creates a favorable environment around us. Beyond that, we need to be taught a profession so individuals can benefit others and earn a respectable living.

Thus, the main thing we need to develop is education, our outlook on life. We need to constantly nurture an environment that will change us for the better, and will let children and adults improve themselves. Alone, we cannot induce any favorable changes in our lives unless society compels them. If society helps and supports a person, if it changes one's values and determines what is good and what is not, that person's desires change accordingly, and he or she will set new personal goals.

It follows that our future depends solely on our choice of environment and how we build it. It's especially so today when we have reached a point where we are completely interdependent and integrally connected throughout the world. Thus, people all over the world determine each other's futures. If a country mistreats another country, or if society treats us in a threatening manner, it affects all our lives and we must act against the adverse influence.

We need to understand that mutual dependence necessitates our building and designing global education. We must first teach ourselves and others that in the end, our futures depend entirely on our environments.

The question of whether or not we have any free choice in our actions is a very important one. Indeed, we see that we don't really have such freedom. Thus far, we've been developing through our drives—the genes we were born with—and through the external environment—parents, kindergarten, school. As grownups, we choose how we will change, but the realization of the change will always take place through the environment, through a more or less selective choice of being under this or that environment. So we do have free choice, but it is actualized only through the environment.

There is an even more important conclusion concerning the new generation or the new era we are in. We are tightly connected and interdependent around the world. The environment has become uniform. For example, if we affect the weather in one place, it could set off an earthquake and tsunami elsewhere. Or if a war breaks out in one place, it immediately affects other areas.

And because we are connected, we needn't simply place ourselves within this or that society, or this or that circle. Rather, we need to set up a general, global, Integral Education for *everyone*. If we are all tied together, we need education and environment as factors that will affect the same values in all of us, so we may understand one another. While we do need to maintain personal freedom, in the end we are so interdependent that we need to understand and to feel one another, to be closer to each other.

Our whole problem is that we don't understand one another. It is just as in a family where there are constant complaints: "He doesn't understand me," or "She doesn't know how I feel." It happens because of incongruence between people. They didn't receive values, insights, outlooks on life that give preference to understanding the *other*, even if he or she is a stranger. That, too, requires education so that the stranger, the other, will not appear to be so alien.

If we are that close and interdependent in every system, whether culture, education, or economy, we must develop global and international education via an international organization. This will ensure that every person in the world has something in common with everyone else—in outlook and in attitudes toward life, culture, and education. That way people will know how to accept and appreciate one another.

This sense of acceptance will make everyone's life safer, and enable us to reach agreements that reflect on international issues, such as politics, economy, and the arms race. It all depends on the way we set up a uniform framework of education for all.

We need to understand that our environment can be the problem, or the solution, to all our problems because *that's the way it is in Nature.* This is why when people harm themselves or society, instead of isolating them in prison, we should place them in a special society that will straighten them out and make them beneficial to society. This is the only gauge by which we should examine how much the environment influences the individual, and accordingly, release the person back into regular society only after the necessary correction has been made.

With children, we should always scrutinize, classify, and match the appropriate environment for each level, age group, character, and tendency. By assessing how different environments influence different individuals, each of us can realize our full potential. We have a versatile tool at our disposal, with numerous types of environments and societies. We should always strive to place people in the particular environment that will help them grow most effectively.

This process is like that of a fruit growing on a tree. It needs certain conditions, such as heat and cold, day and night, moisture and dryness, and a certain blend of minerals to thrive. There are 39 different works to perform on a tree in order for it to bear fruit. The same principle applies to people. We have to influence a person in various ways to produce a good fruit that's sweet for everyone.

This is why the environment is the only element we can use to correct the evil that exists in man and in humanity. We need only take that tool into our hands and set up the environment in a variety of forms and possibilities, according to the culture, education, and customs of the nation and the civilization we wish to correct. This is how we should approach each section of human society in every country, and every person.

In the near future, humanity will rid itself of all redundant occupations, other than those that provide for necessities of life in reasonable conditions. People will work 2-3 hours a day to provide for their necessities, and the rest of the day will be free time.

This free time will be used to design our environments, which will affect us and everyone else. As each of us will affect others, we will take part in trainings so that around each of us will be appropriate influences from several environments and societies in which we will continually grow in the best way.

When we tend to fruits and vegetables in a greenhouse, we provide them with all the conditions they need, and in the right combinations to grow well. The result is a wholesome, sweet fruit. We will have to apply the same process to ourselves and our children. This will be man's primary occupation in the new era.

This is why the crisis is not a negative one, but rather a positive one. It's the birth of a new society, a new humanity. In it, we are beginning to "redesign" ourselves at a new level of connectedness, implementing the full potential that exists in each of us.

We are moving toward bonding and mutual understanding, designing humanity as if it were a single person, with all the organs in that collective image complementing one another. At some point, we will reach a state where all of humanity is as one entity.

Once arrived at that state, we will discover a force in which we feel that we are living out of a collective perception, and not the internal, personal perception of each of us. In such a state, we will experience the lives of others, too; everyone will become close to us, and we will understand them and feel them. We will become integrated with them.

And then life will no longer be an experience of a single individual. Instead, it will be as though we live and breathe along with all of humanity. Thus, we will begin to rise from being small and weak into something great, the greatest in Nature. We will begin to sense life from a new dimension called the "speaking level," as though we are a new species.

At the speaking level, the perception of the world changes from being narrow, personal, and self-centered to a broad and global one. Through our new spectacles we will begin to see the new world as if through the lens of the whole of humanity. When we look at it this way and discover a life that doesn't depend only on ourselves, but on all the people, we will transcend into a sensation of life outside the body.

Through this ascension, we will arrive at something very special. Even now we are living outside our bodies. We live in emotions, desires, and thoughts that we receive from the environment, and which are not our own. Although they are in us, we consider them "outside the body" because we live as we were told we should live, think, feel, and be. We are unaware of how different our perception of the world would be if we lived in a different environment, such as in a forest.

We live within a pattern that society has placed us in while we were growing up and developing, so this is how we see the world. The environment gives us a certain outlook on the world, making us see it in a particular way. Today, it's hard to notice that we're living this way because we're fairly well mingled throughout the world. Yet, we still see how one's values change according to the place of residence. People think differently and therefore look at life differently. They don't see what we see, but perceive reality differently from us.

The problem is that we don't understand one another. Spouses often complain that the other spouse "misunderstands" them. It's true, we don't understand our spouses because we didn't receive the proper education; we were never taught how to lead a family life.

As a youth, for instance, I wasn't taught what it meant to be a woman. Does she also have needs? Does she have her own character? How is her outlook on life different from that of a man? Do I understand her? Do I want to understand her? Am I considerate toward her? Am I even capable of being considerate? After all, a woman's world is completely opposite from that of a man. She is living in a world of her own.

Because boys don't receive any internal patterns for understanding women, they cannot be considerate toward them or understand them. Meetings between them are often collisions: each tries to live beside the other, but neither really understands or mingles with the other. This is a big flaw in our education, as seen in the divorce rates and the number of people who avoid marrying altogether.

The same problem exists when raising children. We don't know how to relate to them. We see how cruelly some parents can treat their children because they don't understand them. A parent is supposed to be an educator, a designer of the child's psyche with which he or she will continue through life. This is why these things *must* be taught.

For tens of thousands of years, we have been evolving by chance. That is, we didn't do anything to direct it. Psychology, the science of human nature, of man's inner world, came into prominence only a hundred or so years ago. Before that, it didn't cross our minds to learn or do anything about how we developed. We evolved just as all animals do—by chance. Only now have we come to a situation where we have no other choice but to study human nature, society, the environment, how to design man, and what we should do with our lives.

Therefore, when talking about life outside the body, we are not referring to anything mystical, but to values and outlooks we receive from others. When we can see the world through the eyes of others, we can understand them. This is what we need to learn.

It's very hard for men to perceive the world through the eyes of a woman, but because we are still leading family lives, we must lead good family lives. We have to prepare our children for life and help them understand the psychology of the opposite sex, not just how to live together, but how to enjoy the experience.

Through this mingling, we will acquire another half of the world. When we acquire an addition outside our own bodies, this is called "living outside the body." This is how we build ourselves.

Until today, we've been evolving *within* our bodies, in a life as self-centered as possible, satisfying ourselves as much as possible and ignoring other's views, minds, and outlooks as much as we could. Today, the crisis we all face is forcing us to mingle with others and acquire their perspectives, or their "interiors," as though we were going out of ourselves and beginning to mingle with others.

By doing so, we will come to perceive the capabilities of the rest of the world: their desires and thoughts. I thus become like the rest of the world, as if exiting my own body and truly acquiring an ability to feel the whole of reality.

A place for a new dimension has been opened here, a place for a completely new sensation—to see and feel reality not through my personal, narrow perception, but through collective sensations and perceptions: an accumulation of all the people.

When I draw closer to others, I become educated by the entirety of this rich society. I acquire the ability to see life through multifaceted emotions and intellects, not just my own, but through the others within me. I become included in this group and see a far richer world than I do now. It is called "life outside the body," outside my current ego.

There is a special opportunity here for each of us to expand our emotional and intellectual perceptions. If I'm a part of others, feeling what they feel and thinking what they think, I will expand my abilities many times over.

Our perception of everything depends entirely on the number of discernments we make of everything, and on the resolution. The number of discernments depends on the extent to which we consist of opposites, the contrast that we detect in things, and the ways we can use them as building blocks, like Lego bricks.

Thus, we analyze what everything is made of and how this complexity differs from other complexities. When I absorb emotions from others and they become included in me, I am enriched. I become a collection of opposites, by which I begin to perceive the world in such a versatile manner that, compared to my previous, superficial perception, it's as if I have shifted to another perception.

This is truly the psychology of a new perception, a new world. With it, we transcend the limitations of the body, the boundaries of time, motion, and place, because we have become included with all humanity, acquiring the collective emotions and perceptions of the whole of humanity, a single intelligence operating in the whole of humanity.

We begin by being included with others and discovering their collective feelings and perceptions, which actually come to us from Nature. We have the ability to reach what is hidden inside of Nature, that "heart and mind" from which all developments in this world arise. By so developing, we return to that same place, the root from which the whole chain of still, vegetative, animate, and the speaking (us), emerged. We return to the beginning of evolution and thus complete the circle.

It is with good reason that Nature is urging us toward mutual connection, almost to the point of losing our individuality. In truth, we're not losing it; we're rising above it! Our individuality is corporeal, animal, and only a concern for the body so it can exist as comfortably as possible for whatever time it's given. But the purpose of our evolution is to rise above our concern for the personal body, and move into a general concern. That general concern gives us entirely different tools for living from outside the body. This is why it is called "exiting my own body."

By rising above the ego into general concern, I discover the design and purpose of Creation, Nature's intention. Here, nothing evolves by chance, but all occurs according to a plan. I become able to see the plan the minute I rise into integral vision, when I begin to connect myself to others. This is when I begin to perceive that integral vision. It's as if I have changed my glasses into "round" glasses, integral ones, where I can see the whole of Nature.

It is not that I receive from Nature anything for my own body, such as food or rest. I am past that level. Now, I look at life regardless of my body. I look at Nature as if I'm not in my body. I judge, examine, and scrutinize life with the mind and heart of the whole of humanity. It is a completely different degree from the one at which I currently exist.

At present, I'm just like any other animal. I may be slightly more developed, but it's uncertain whether it's for better or for worse. But when mingling with the whole of humanity, I arrive at a new dimension, I qualitatively change my perception of the world I am in, and that change becomes my real world. I don't look out at life through my narrow, selfish crevice, seeing what is to my benefit so I may pull it in through a crack in the wall—some food, some rest, some other pleasures, and that's it.

Instead, I go out through that crack and live outside, in the world. And there, in the world outside, the outlook is completely different. It is no longer through an egoistic filter of "What's good for me?" where all I see are either what is good for me or what might harm me. Rather, I see the world *regardless of me.* This is called the "new dimension," the "speaking dimension." I discover the "mind and heart" that exist in that enlightened state outside my body, outside this wall. I come out through the crack and discover the entire process, the very purpose of Creation.

Currently, we only discover a fraction of what might be beyond that wall, like the dark matter in the universe. Yet, although we cannot ordinarily perceive it, the dark matter constitutes over 90% of all the matter in the universe. Likewise, we have not discovered the inclusive mind and heart of the universe.

Scientists often talk about it, however. Cosmologists say that this mind and heart is something huge, but we can't feel it. It's like sounds we can't hear with our natural senses because they come from a dimension above our own. And yet, through our new, global senses we will discover that dimension.

To summarize, we can divide the process we are going through into two stages. The first is what we have been going through thus far, evolving quite randomly without using the environment to monitor our growth. But now that we've entered the next stage, we feel that we have no other choice but to evolve in a different manner, toward a certain direction. We feel that we must become integral and global, connected as one individual with one heart with the rest of humanity.

This, in fact, is "the speaking degree." We obtain that degree using the right environment, by which we transcend the animate degree—our incidental lives—and begin to aim ourselves toward becoming a handsome fruit, nurtured in a greenhouse until it ripens to perfection.

Thus, we see that everything depends on the environment, and our only problem is how to set up such a diverse environment that is also suitable for everyone, so that all can be educated through it, express themselves in the best, most appropriate way, and be connected to others in the integral system.

We need to examine people only according to their willingness to be included in a good society and thus "design" themselves. Our purpose is only to see how to provide each of us with a good environment, ignoring what kinds of people we currently may be, but focusing on building a good environment henceforth.

As we build the environment, we will see how much we affect one another, how much we do or do not understand one another, how much we can change society and the environment, and how much our relationships with others change their behavior and moods.

Through this new, Integral Education, we will know how to build our environment so it brings us into unity, wherein each of us will find his or her perfect expression. This is why we emphasize the environment as the cause of our best future, and hope this idea will be accepted all over the world, for the well-being of all of humanity.

CHAPTER FOUR

One Law Affects All

WHAT WE MUST DO
TO BE SUITABLE TO NATURE

Over time, the still, vegetative, animate, and human levels were created and gradually evolved. We evolved from generation to generation, from year to year, and even from day to day. If we examine the way we progress in life, we will see that there seems to be a rule here, a mechanism that develops the whole of Nature toward greater complexity and interconnectedness among its parts. All parts of reality, everything we see on Earth, continue developing in the same direction. It seems as though there is a single law that operates within us and compels us to develop in one direction. And whether we want it or not, we are compelled to act according to its commands. Therefore, we must study that general law that is in all of Nature, a law that includes us and affects us.

In scientific research, we study Nature's laws, and knowing them yields success. We learn how to avoid bad situations, how to advance toward good ones, and how to avoid mistakes. Therefore, we should know that general law, which includes within it all the laws of physics, chemistry, biology, zoology, botany, astronomy, and those affecting the human body and human psychology. The more we can understand this law, of which we still know very little, the more positive impact it will have on us.

Science helps us improve our lives and make them more convenient. Previously, a man had to toil from dawn to dusk to be able to survive. Today, thanks to advanced technology, one person can produce food for thousands of people. And this is true not just in food production, but also in construction, textile, hi-tech, education, and culture, to name just a few areas. Humanity has so advanced that today relatively few people can provide the whole of humanity with a good, reasonable, problem-free life.

There is, however, one problem: *Man is a natural-born egoist.* This is why we can't utilize our vast potential, the abilities we obtain by knowing Nature's laws. While abundance exists, few possess power, money, and instruments. As a result, many don't receive even the most basic needs to sustain themselves. In other words, there is *one cause* for which we cannot build a peaceful, good, convenient, safe, and healthy life on this beautiful, flourishing planet: the self-centered human nature.

This is why we need to study human nature and find the right way to work with it. We must learn how we can make our lives good, how we can correct our nature so we make life good and convenient for ourselves and *for others.*

We are only now beginning to understand that the whole problem is man's self-centered nature. This realization stems from our discovery of the general law that is only now being revealed to us: the Law of the Global Force, the force that contains within it all other forces. Whether we want it or not—and we usually don't—that force is leading us toward more connectedness and toward becoming more needy of each other.

Scientists write that the direction of the Law of Evolution, the law that develops us, is to bring us into one form, in which we are so connected that we will feel that each person is actually dependent upon the whole of humanity, and the whole of humanity is dependent upon each person. This reality may seem far off, but it's already clear that this is the direction we're headed.

Yet, for now, this law contradicts our nature. We aren't built to accept it because each of us thinks only of him or herself, not comprehending that we are all interdependent. If we understood it and felt it, if we really saw that we were dependent on and connected to everyone else, we would first want to make sure everyone was happy and that everyone related to me favorably.

The problem is that we don't see how "round" and connected the world is. This is why we are in such a crisis, which forcefully detaches us from the life we've grown accustomed to over the past decades. We've grown accustomed to working long hours, making money, wasting it, and producing things that aren't needed, just so we can sell them. We accumulate possessions and money trying to build a safety net—pension, healthcare, house, savings—to be sure that at the end of our lives, we and our children will not be lacking anything.

It's clear where we want to go, but it seems that the direction we've been on has been wrong. Nature is shattering our plans. Even the wealthy among us can't make that dream come true, much less the middle class and below, which are the majority of humanity. In fact, Nature is leading us in the *opposite* direction—toward finding safety, prosperity, and development in *good connections* between us.

Through the channel of forging good relationships, we will receive everything we want, and not by each of us trying to hold on to his or her good private life. We can clearly see the change coming from the all-encompassing crisis that's happening now, which is shattering all the previous rules.

The crisis is showing us that we are in a new world. For the first time, instead of many different, seemingly disparate and disconnected laws of Nature, we are beginning to sense that a new law is operating upon us. All of a sudden we are all under its umbrella, and all of us are drawn in the same direction.

There has never been a state in the history of humanity when so many different countries were facing a similar situation. Everywhere—North America, South America, Europe, Africa, Asia, Siberia, and even in Australia and New Zealand—everyone is in the same process of decline. Regardless of society, civilization, religion, or the environment we are in, a great cloud has suddenly descended upon us, enveloping us all together.

As scientists are discovering, and as we are feeling through the crisis and the connections among us, we are all dependent on one another. The "butterfly effect" is acting in such a way that through connections with six people, every person knows every other person in the world! Today there are studies proving that even our thoughts are affecting the climate—that earthquakes and tsunamis depend on human relationships and on people's ways of life. It turns out that we are facing *one law that is forcing us to unite.*

Thus, to have a better life, we must contemplate how to move *toward* that law rather than *away* from it. We must want to unite, to advance in a good, wholesome, comfortable direction, to move in harmony with the laws of Nature, not against them. Otherwise Nature's way will win—and will, undoubtedly, break us.

The laws of Nature are unchanging. These aren't political laws that we can bend however we want. The laws of Nature are *above* us. Just as we can only study the laws of physics, chemistry, and biology in order to know how to use them properly, the laws of Nature are absolute. It follows that we *have* to study the singular law, the Law of Comprehensive Unity, and join it to the best of our ability, as that Law of Comprehensive Unity is the general law of the whole of Nature.

Therefore, what should we change within us so we are more congruent with Nature? When we are in that state, we feel no pressure from Nature. Such pressure can manifest in various ways, such as severe weather, earthquakes, diseases, wars, and divorces.

The search for the answer to the question from the previous paragraph leads us into the study of human nature. Human nature is a desire to live, to feel good, to enjoy. That is, we constantly want to satisfy something within us called "desire." When we want to sleep, we want to satisfy a desire for rest. When we want to eat, we want to satisfy a desire for food, and so on.

Human desires divide into several basic categories: food, sex, family, money, respect, power (domination), and knowledge. All other desires are actually "sub-desires" within those categories. All our desires are generally called "desires to enjoy," a desire to be satisfied. If I understand that it's in my best interest to bond with others through those desires so we are all in congruence with the force of Nature, that singular law, then I must correct every desire in me so it acts to connect with others.

Thus, I must aim those desires so they are for everyone's benefit. If I try to satisfy only my own desire, it is considered an "egoistic desire." If I aim each of my desires to benefit all of us *together*, then I must take *everyone* into account and *think of all as one*, like that singular law that is compelling me. Therefore, I must aim each desire within me toward *everyone's benefit*.

The question is, "How should that be done?"

Scientists, economists, psychologists, sociologists, as well as our own experiences tell us that we no longer have a choice but to care for one another and act as a single organism. Yet, my own nature thinks otherwise. It thinks that I should first receive for myself, satisfy my own wants and not care for others. And if it decides to care for others, it's for my own benefit.

But it's not enough to be content. In a corrected family, I don't think like that; I think of the entire family as one, instead of conditioning my behavior for my own benefit. Also, the Law of the Global Force is compelling us to grow accustomed to thinking of everyone as one unit, to think of the world as a single family.

To do that, each of us must help the others, thus building together a system of new, Integral Education, which will connect us and show us that we really have no other choice.

Thus, how can we unite?

There is another special law in Nature by which we can come closer to each other and overcome our egos. It is called "Habit Becomes Second Nature." We know that to achieve satisfactory results, we often repeat certain actions several times. We exercise the action until it becomes a habit for us. However, the chances of it becoming a habit depend on the extent to which the environment compels us to do it, on the extent to which everyone else is doing it, and on the degree to which the act is supported by everything we see around us.

Therefore, if we set up the education and a supportive environment for each of us, we will be able to advance toward a state where a person is impressed by how people are thoughtful of others. We can do this by affecting public opinion through the media and through explanations.

We must purposely pretend to others to be good, thoughtful of others, just like a family, and show that we care for others as much as for ourselves. We have to keep this act going *all the time*, carry ourselves about as though we were already a corrected society.

Gradually, through exercising such behavior, through public opinion, and through the influence of the environment, we will actually begin to think in that direction. We will be impressed by it so much, we will acquire an internal habit that we can no longer do without. Thus, although we will have absorbed that habit from the outside, having been forced to take it on ourselves, it will become our nature just like the nature with which we were born.

This is why it is imperative that we use the law, "Habit Becomes Second Nature." It depends on the extent to which we are under our own pressure and social pressures to remember the game, and thus advance.

You could say that we are acting as kids here. They, too, imagine that they are doing something important, that they are building something, while we know it is a game and not for real. The kids make mistakes in their games, rebuild, then break them down and build again. But precisely through those games they learn and understand.

Without games, a child would grow up savage, like a young animal that grows into a mature animal. This is why psychologists and other professionals build special systems for children's games from various materials and in different forms. This is the only way we can advance.

Even our physical development would be impossible without games. We call them "sports." Sports are games where we accustom ourselves through various exercises to do things that we wouldn't be able to do without practice (games), meaning continuous repetition of the same act. Indeed, we can accomplish great things through habits.

We can also see that people who live together feel one another and understand one another even without words. It's like an internal discourse, the result of habit, because by living under the same roof and feeling one another, they become "included," mingling with one another. In the past, entire nations and civilizations were built this way, by mingling people who were strangers until they acquired the characteristics of a nation.

In other words, the law, "Habit Becomes Second Nature," is made especially for us. With this law, even from our undesirable and unnatural forms, we will come to a state where we assume the forms we have chosen *against* our nature and turn them into the new form that is already within us. This is how we advance and build ourselves.

We are born with only an egoistic desire to enjoy, not caring for anything but ourselves, like a newborn baby that feels only itself and thinks only of itself. It takes several weeks for a baby to begin to feel the world outside it, to really see and hear, to "switch on" its senses. But what it wants from life, from the environment, is for its needs to be satisfied, primarily through its mother. This is how we grow.

We need to understand that we deliberately received the egoistic desire we were born with so we could build atop it a form different from our original nature, an altruistic form of giving and bonding using the law, "Habit Becomes Second Nature."

Yet, we are opposite from that. We are individualists. Each of us wants to profit from others, to be completely inconsiderate of others. Hence, we are constantly conflicting with and colliding with each other.

Nature has deliberately created this negative form within us so that from it we would build the positive, good form, one of connection among us. We will use all the powers at our disposal and build that new form consciously and with complete comprehension. We will reach a state where we are all connected in similarity to the general Law of Nature, which is all bestowal, goodness, and love.

Then we will understand that this law is not evil, that all the forces we currently feel as blows are not bad forces. The disintegrating families, drugs, terrorism, fear of a nuclear world war, ecological and financial crises, and all the forces that seem negative to us are intended only to make us build our forces of love, giving, and bonding. Anything that happens to us that we currently feel as a negative force affecting us is sensed in us as negative only because we are opposite from the singular law.

For example, when we are faced with heatstroke or hypothermia, we need to know what to do to balance our temperature and bring it back to normal. When the body is under pressure, such as when diving, or if we climb to altitudes where there is little oxygen, we create a kind of "compensation" that brings us back to balance with Nature.

Today we are suffering blows from every direction. Every day, humanity is being pressed together under the collective blows landing on it. Is there an instrument we can use to balance ourselves with Nature?

Everything that happens to us is an expression of our oppositeness from Nature. Therefore, we have to compensate for that oppositeness. Nature is presenting us with adverse phenomena, but if we overcome ourselves and correct ourselves, becoming as similar to Nature as we can, we will experience those very forces as positive because we will be in balance with them. At that point, all the crises—climate, family relations, international relations, and economic crises—will calm down and we will discover a good, wholesome life in every way.

How do we play that game? We learned that Nature is a singular force that operates on all of us, that it "wants" us to learn how to balance ourselves because then we will begin to comprehend the whole of reality. By bonding, we will understand where we truly are. We can obtain that bonding by cultivating good relationships. Although we might not yet want these relationships, we can create them through games, using the law, "Habit Becomes Second Nature."

To realize the bonding between us in actual fact, we need to create the bonding within society through our attitudes toward it. We must build social systems where each person feels obliged to treat society favorably, where the well-being of society, as well as one's own well-being, depends on one's attitude toward society.

If we wish to restructure man's attitude toward society—because we are dependent on each other and society demands that each us treats it properly—we need to understand what society needs to do *de facto*. For that, society must give us *examples* of the right behavior, like that of a mother toward her child. Society must fundamentally transform its impact on each of us, beginning with transforming the media and the educational system. These must provide each of us with a sense of urgency to change our attitudes toward one another.

A good society is like an incubator, enveloping and warming its young, a place where we develop well and properly. Just as temperature, humidity, and all the conditions in an incubator are ideal for the hatchling to develop in the egg in the best, quickest, and healthiest way, we need to build around us a society that will be our own ideal incubator. In such a society we will be warm, cozy, comfortable, and we will never want to leave it. Just as a fetus develops in its mother's womb in the safest way because the womb is perfectly suited for it, we must establish our society so everyone develops ideally in it.

In such an incubator, each person builds the society for his own, as well as for everybody else's sake. When everyone works that way for everyone else, we will build our great family and all will become kin.

It turns out that our attitude toward Nature, toward that singular law by which we should be as one, is realized within our society. In fact, our attitude toward society and the realization of that law within it is more important than our attitude toward Nature itself! The single most important thing for us to do is to construct our human environment. For this reason, everyone must learn these new studies and acquire a new career: Becoming a Human Being in the New Society.

To master this new profession of "being humane," each of us must rise to a level where he or she completely understands what is happening in Nature, what is happening within us, and how we should relate to others. Studies show that the minute this awareness begins to affect all the members of a society, no one can escape it. It feeds each person good nourishment, and we change whether we want to or not. Just as children change through society by simply watching examples of others, we are educated and acquire new modes of behavior, attitude, and values simply through observing examples from society.

We will no longer count our desires, whether for food, sex, family, money, respect, power, and knowledge, or the hundreds of other desires derived from them. We will not trouble our minds with the desires themselves, but instead with how we use them, meaning with our *intention* toward society when we use them. What's important is our intention when we use the "self," the desires. We need to transform the use of our abilities to be *favorable for society.*

When we do, our individual sense of "me" becomes "we," and the "we," which is seemingly a collection of individuals, becomes "one"—"one" that is in bonding, in balance with the singular law that organizes us, and which is in a positive connection with us.

Thus, a human being truly becomes humane, one who understands one's overall nature. On the way toward it, he or she learns many psychological rules and all the rules of reality. Thus, one becomes included with all that exists in Nature and achieves the highest degree—that of the singular force that operates on us and draws us toward it in a manner that currently appears to us as a crisis.

In fact, we are in the midst of a bubble that is compelling us to change. We are surrounded from all sides and we have nowhere to run. Today we are increasingly discovering that one law operates on all the elements at every level— the overall Law of Balance in a global-integral system. It is called, "Nature."

The concept of "Nature" relates to all the laws operating in the degrees of still, vegetative, animate, and human levels. All the laws belonging to the global-integral system are under a single law, the Law of Balance, otherwise known as "homeostasis," and all of Nature is drawn toward it.

That law exists in physics, too. Everything is drawn toward calm, motionlessness, comfort, a static state, minimal entropy, and minimal spending of energy. If one point is warm and another is cold, the gap between them will gradually disappear until they equalize. This is "pressure equality." This is how it works in Nature—it is the general law in Nature, and we humans should follow suit. That is, we, too, should become balanced, as is Nature.

This is why the crisis we are experiencing today is on the human level. It compels us to see that we are all connected in a single system, that we all are parts of Nature, albeit Nature on the human level. Many scientists and academics already see the world as global and integral, and recognize that we are living in a holistic world (from the word, "whole"). There is only one Nature. Accordingly, all the sciences—physics, chemistry, biology, and zoology—are connected to each other.

Every substance consists of elements, which are in turn comprised of atoms. The various connections among the atoms create different materials. Although there are many materials, there is only one force operating on all the levels—still vegetative, animate, and human. In atoms and molecules, that force acts as an attracting or repelling force. In humans, it is the force that expands or contracts the lungs and the heart, or creates contradictions between fact and fiction. There are always two conflicting forces acting against each other. Yet, they are operated by the single force that balances them, for the whole of Nature strives toward balance.

Man needs tools that will allow him to see that the world is round, that everyone depends on everyone else, that all are subject to one influence, and that they must obey a single law. This is the outlook on life, the philosophy, psychology, and information that we are meant to acquire for the rest of our lives. Until we begin to study and comprehend this law, our lives will seem miserable to us; we won't know the kind of world we are preparing for our children and grandchildren, and we won't understand why we are here in the first place.

To perceive our interdependence, we need a good environment that will influence us. We can see the effects of society from life, from education, and from just about anything we do. Through a good environment, we can provide a remedy before illness breaks out, since any negative impact from Nature comes because we are not synchronized with it or with the environment. Each blow we experience testifies to a state of imbalance.

Hence, as I need to wear something warm when I am cold, I must counteract any imbalance. If the environment affects us, then we must create an environment where we affect each other positively. We will oblige everyone to behave kindly to each other, and expel anyone who resists that behavior. After all, we want to lead a *good* life. We want everyone to have food, a home, a family, health care, savings for old age, vacations, things we all need.

If we want it to be this way, we have a chance to build a society where all care for all. Yet, this can only be in an environment where we treat each other well. This kindness may be compulsory, but by getting used to acting out good relationships and accepting that behavior as law, we will get used to it and it will become our nature.

Until today we were "savages" wishing to "consume" one another. Henceforth, if we behave favorably toward each other, we will turn ourselves inside out. In time, we won't be so savage anymore, but more "humane," and humanity will be entirely different.

When we are in balance with Nature, new opportunities will open up to us: we will sense Nature, discover new things, develop new abilities, build new instruments, and revolutionize our world because we will know the laws of Nature by becoming similar to it. We will become like the rest of reality. We will act out because we won't have a choice, and we will establish good relations with others.

Nature knows precisely how to develop every creature in the best way for its balance with its environment. It is the Law of Evolution, and now it is affecting humankind, as well. That law has a plan, a formula of development activated by the Law of Evolution. Nature has a plan for the future to bring each desire, at each stage, to the ideal development for balance with the environment.

To summarize, according to the plan embedded within Nature, we are to rise and develop, stage by stage. Also, each stage must be more developed than its predecessor. For that, we must know both stages. Therefore, how do we, as a human society, raise ourselves from the current stage into the next one, in which we are happy and balanced with the environment?

Evolution as we know it is coming to a conclusion, and we must choose our own best future form, and then bring ourselves to it. This is why the crisis we are in is unique, for it requires human intervention. We must grow, perceive Nature—its law and direction—and build our development by ourselves, using the environment. Nature is merely stimulating within us desires so we cannot put off or avoid developing.

Put differently, to resolve the crisis we must know our next state, study it, comprehend it, feel its necessity, and construct by ourselves the Nature that will compel us to develop toward the right form. It is possible because now *we* must act, instead of Nature. That is, we mustn't let ourselves be goaded into developing from behind, wherein Nature will develop us according to its reason and plan. Today we must take the plan into our own hands, acquire the knowledge, build the forces of development, the system of development, the incubator mentioned earlier, and grow.

If we learn how to be "human," we will reach the best, most comfortable, safest, and healthiest possible state. Therefore, we must be thankful for the situation and the time that we are in, both of which are admitting us into the new era, into a world that is all good.

If we begin to actualize that singular law within us, in a few short weeks we will feel how it operates, how habit becomes second nature, and that we can no longer live in bad relationships with each other. And should we lose it and forget, we'll be reminded of the time we were together, united, when everyone felt one another, and how wonderful and desirable that state was. Thus, that state will draw us back to it.

Let's hope that with mutual support we will be able to reach a state where "acting out" the habit will lead us into good nature, into love.

CHAPTER FIVE

All Tied Up

IS INTERDEPENDENCE A FACT?

All the systems—in Nature, in human society, and in our personal lives—exist under mutual influence. In fact, the whole of Nature acts as a single mechanism. The more we study the universe, the more we discover that all its systems are interdependent. The planets circle the sun, and most have moons circling them. This is a vast system, and the more we study it, the more we see that its elements are moving reciprocally. They are so interdependent that our moon, for instance, affects everything that happens on Earth—our health, our feelings, the water movements in the oceans, and many other changes. The sun also affects us. Each solar flare affects us, and some flares even pose hazards to electronic and communication systems on Earth.

Earth itself is a ball of fire burning from within. We are practically living on the thin, fragile crust of a volcano. Yet, everything maintains a very subtle balance. Biologists, zoologists, and botanists all say that to create a life such as we have on Earth requires very special conditions that have not been found anywhere else in the universe. The existence of life requires very specific conditions, which have to act in harmony: gravity, the right amount of water, pressures, temperature, and many other elements. These conditions combine into a complex formula that allows for the creation of life-sustaining biosphere only if that formula is followed to the letter.

Climate is another example of external elements that affect our lives. We can predict the weather with reasonable accuracy up to a week in advance. The complexity of formulas taking into account temperature, moisture, air pressure, wind, and other elements requires very powerful computers because meteorologists must consider the weather all over the world. This creates the huge amount of data required simply to predict tomorrow's temperature, wind speed, and height of waves.

Yet, this information is necessary because we are no longer sedentary. We move around using different types of vehicles, and therefore need to know the weather in, and on the way to our destinations.

The weather is a good example of the tight links between the still level, which affects the vegetative, which affects the animate, which affects us humans. We also see how Man affects those elements in the chain. Our lives depend on the still level because we live on the produce of the land. We are dependent on the vegetative level because it is our agriculture and creates oxygen for us. Likewise, we are dependent on the animate level because we are living creatures that need food, without which we will not survive.

We humans can survive only within a society in which each of us performs a certain role, and with that role takes up a specific place in the human mosaic. Moreover, we are becoming an increasingly complex society, where we are *increasingly dependent on one another*. We transfer funds from bank to bank, from continent to continent, and we send ships with various cargos to every corner of the world.

If, for instance, I examine the shirt I'm wearing, I will find that numerous countries took part making it—the raw materials, processing them, sewing, selling, shipping, and so forth.

We are already used to this interdependence and take it for granted, but for now it is primarily commercial and doesn't require any emotional participation on our part. However, lately we have begun to see that the connections among us have reached such depths that require more thorough participation on our part.

We are already so tied together that anything that happens in one country immediately affects its neighbors. This is why today countries interfere with other countries' internal affairs, and may even demand the replacement of the government, as if those countries weren't sovereign states.

An example of such a case is Syria. Countries from all over the world are criticizing it and are trying to put an end to the killing of civilians through political and economic sanctions. That involvement demonstrates that our interdependence obliges all of us to care for one another.

The connections among us are so tight that they demand effective international mechanisms of trade, science, and culture, without which we won't be able to exist. If we want to have a good life, we must develop very similar cultures, education, and approaches to life throughout the world.

For example, over the past several decades, tourism has evolved tremendously and today we regularly travel from country to country. It is no coincidence that countries have become much closer to each other in their way of life and worldview. We are all fed by the same TV networks and news broadcasts, and we've had virtual connections over the Internet for approximately 20 years now. Soon we will even be able to communicate without any language barriers using simultaneous interpretation programs. Thus, even those who don't understand English, the international language, will be able to communicate with everyone else.

Studies indicate that today we are so connected that through six people, any person is connected to any other person on Earth. It is almost as if we're holding hands with the entire world.

Today, countries cannot do whatever they want even in their own territories because they might change the balance of Earth's interior, which will affect not only its neighbors, but even remote countries. This is why countries made agreements on various topics, such as the Kyoto Protocol that determined quotas for the emission of greenhouse gases.

Today, almost every country has its own quota for fishing, for emission of greenhouse gases, and for every other natural resource we use. In other words, we are beginning to grasp that we have only one Earth to live on, that it is our common home, and in it, we all depend on one another. Therefore, we can't do whatever we want on this planet.

Regrettably, we are still evolving. We are still in an egoistic stage where we are not so considerate of each other. One example to this self-centeredness is the race to dominate space. We send all kinds of spaceships into space and have already caused significant disorders there. There are numerous "lumps" of different sizes, known as "space junk," floating lifelessly in space. These pieces could fall down and cause damage, or collide with a spaceship on its way to or from Earth.

There have also been some unpleasant natural phenomena lately, such as the volcanic eruption in Iceland, affecting all of Europe all the way to Siberia, and shutting down the majority of airports on the continent. Likewise, the March 2011 tsunami that hit the nuclear power station in Fukushima, Japan, affected the entire world, made everyone rethink the construction of nuclear power stations and contemplate the closing of existing ones.

Clearly, today no country can establish its interior policy, much less its foreign policy without considering tens or even hundreds of external elements. With every potential move, each country must consider its impact on the entire world. This is true even for the strongest countries, which also have to calculate their measures because we are all interdependent, and any change in one country could affect all the others.

Each day, we can feel more vividly that we are living in an increasingly complicated and interdependent world. This is why it is possible to speak of a common law affecting all of us: the "Law of Mutual Guarantee." That law affects not only countries, international corporations, and international relations, but *every person* is subject to its impact.

This impact grows clearer each year. Thus, if a bank in Europe or America falters, every other country will feel it, too, especially China and India, which produce and sell their products to these continents. Likewise, a problem in China will affect half the world. Economy, finance, and commerce have tied us together to the point that maintaining contact has become vital for our survival because our food, clothing, heating, medicine, electronics, and every other industry depend on it.

Today there isn't a country in the world that provides for its own needs. A hundred years ago, each country was almost entirely self-sufficient. But since England conquered India and decided that it was easier to import fruits and vegetables from India rather than grow them by itself, a major shift occurred. Instead of agriculture, the British developed industry, and imported their food from India.

People began to understand that differentiation was worthwhile, allowing for higher quality and lower production costs for each product, enabling people to buy from one another what they didn't manufacture at lower costs and better quality than if they made them themselves. Initially, each factory manufactured almost everything, from the nuts and bolts to the complete machine. Even the electricity to keep the factory working was produced "in house."

Afterwards, industry began to divide production among different factories: one made nuts and bolts, another made metal parts, another still produced electrical parts, and so on. Today, producing a car requires a supply chain from thousands of places and numerous countries.

In recent years this phenomenon has become even more expansive. Thus, today Japanese cars are manufactured anywhere from the U.S. to India, with the Japanese running operations from long distance. Sometimes they aren't even Japanese cars because even the managers are not Japanese, and all that remains is the brand name.

As a result, there is such confusion in every area that, for the most part, we cannot tell which manufacturer produced what and where. In many countries we can see many different plants, sometimes even gas stations or fast food stands, from other countries. Today, in each industry there are foreign owners that join in for the business. Governments don't interfere with the process because they profit from it: the citizens have jobs, the government collects its taxes, and everyone benefits.

Once the developed countries progressed sufficiently, they began to develop other countries in the "third world"—Africa and Asia. They built plants and factories for which it was necessary to educate the locals, which is how schools were established in those countries, while Western countries began to take students from those countries into European universities.

In this way, the world became connected through education, culture, science, and industry. The global connections became so strong that Americans used to joke that "to make a phone call from New York to Boston, you had to go through the communication center in India." Thus, communication lines connect throughout the world, making distance and location irrelevant.

If we look deeper we will see that our entire planet is connected through a vast, diverse, and multilayered network. Today it is impossible to do anything without obtaining the equipment, knowledge, and human resources for it from around the world.

And yet, today the global network isn't working as it should. There are many reasons for this, and sociologists, experts in political science, and economists all have their views. But at the end of the day there is only one reason for our social dysfunction: our connections have become so strong, they require that we deepen our connections with each other.

To continue our development, we must bond more closely so we can understand the concept of "mutual guarantee." We must come to realize that we are all interdependent because we are all living on the same planet, and we have no other choice but to feel just like a single family.

Our development started when we began to trade and send one another machines, food, and clothing. Subsequently, we began to collaborate in manufacturing, finally establishing the World Bank and other international financial entities. Stock markets began to use computers and the Internet, and today people can trade in Tokyo, Germany, Moscow, and New York without moving from their desks because all stock markets work the same way. All one needs to do is decide where and how much to invest.

Moreover, money doesn't have to actually be transferred anywhere. It is wired electronically. The money itself could be placed in any country in the world; what counts is the money transfer orders being emailed and wired around the world.

As we have said, lately we've been sensing that the connections among us cannot continue as before. We can see it very clearly in Europe: On the one hand, this is a developed continent, but on the other hand, it is the most segregated of all. There is a lack of congruence among countries, filling them with misunderstandings and mistrust because people cannot fully grasp that they all belong to the same system.

They must realize that it's not enough to retain a common market merely for economic needs. Rather, it is important to unite countries through a much closer connection. They must be closer in spirit, in perception of their situations, in recognizing that they cannot do without that union.

Herein, however, lies the difficulty. Now, all twenty-seven EU nations have to learn that interdependence among them is necessary. The problem is that although decision-makers, politicians, scientists, and ordinary people understand the situation, they are still reluctant to give up their national pride.

However, they don't need to relinquish their ways of life, habits, culture, or folklore. Instead, they need to rise *above* those differences and connect with each other in mutual guarantee. Although we are different, we must behave as a family.

Admittedly, this isn't simple. For instance, if I have parents and so does my wife, and these parents have other children, and both she and I have brothers and sisters, as well as our own children, somehow we must be considerate of one another because, for better and for worse, we depend on one another. We have no intention to change ourselves, nor do we intend to force change on anybody else. We understand that we are all different, that we all have our priorities, yet we are determined to live together.

By this joint decision, we actually agree, even if nonverbally, to build our lives together, recognizing that it may not always be a rose garden. We realize that we may have to make concessions and compromises, but we connect in order to build our families, the future generation, and for that we must support one another.

That education, which prepares us for living together, is missing in today's young couples. They are not taught how to get along despite differences and disagreements. While we have the freedom to choose our partners, our choices often fail.

The lack of education concerning how to live together makes disintegration of families and divorces a serious problem. Half the world's population, especially the young, either stays single until late in life, or chooses to never marry or have kids. They see that they cannot even take care of themselves, much less assume responsibility for others. This crisis, which began some thirty years ago, is only worsening.

We can compare the situation in today's families to the situation among countries. Each country is both a receiver and a giver in terms of its relationships with other countries. Therefore, in diplomacy, too, we must learn how to make concessions and how to unite beyond differences and gaps. We've never been taught how to make concessions, but in the end, only by compromising can we expect anything good to transpire.

We are currently in the midst of a crisis that is teaching us the necessity of mutual guarantee, where we become each other's "guarantors." We are hopeful that this necessity will be sensed in all humanity and will not end in a "divorce" because a divorce among countries means war. We need to understand that we have no choice but to show restraint with each other. That was why the UN was established—to be a place where nations could seemingly unite and discuss peace.

This is also why many other organizations have been established, addressing topics such as education and health. I was once in Geneva to give a series of lectures, and was surprised by the vast number of organizations that exist there. Entire streets are covered with headquarters of organizations, some of which I'd never heard of. One organization allots radio and television frequencies to the entire world so that stations will not interfere with each other's broadcasts. Another organization sets standards for medicine production. Another health organization determines health standards, and promotes cooperation among countries, in favor of the patients. There is even an organization that determines the colors of countries' flags to avoid using the same colors by more than one country.

These organizations set standards on every imaginable topic because countries have become so interconnected and close that common rules must be created for all of them. Just as the parliament of each country determines rules in favor of the whole country, to enable modern life to continue, rules must be determined for the whole world. Without those international organizations, which have existed for decades, it would be very difficult for us to maintain global order.

What's important today is not to define the territory of each country, as in the past. Now we are in a situation where we must build a "common roof" for all the nations. That "roof" means we must come to understand and feel that we are all together, seemingly in the same room. In this room, it will be very difficult to stay together unless we form a bond, a good connection. Within that connection, we must come to feel close to one another; we must feel such interdependence that it will compel us to change our attitudes toward each other.

That picture, which we can already see before us, clearly demonstrates how interdependent we really are, whether we like it or not. We are interdependent in food, clothing, education, culture, technology, industry, energy, water, and power. We are even interdependent in air because if someone doesn't keep air pollution regulations, it could pollute the air worldwide.

The organizations of the international community are very important because they give us a sense of mutual dependence that is far more complete than that of family members. In a family, one person may be angry with another and even stop talking to that person or disconnect all ties. Among countries, there is no such prerogative. The hundreds of countries around the globe are set up in a "mosaic" from which none can escape. We can see that each time a country wishes to act independently, it fails, and after some time the country abandons the idea.

Sometimes countries do perform such acts of separation, but it is more verbal than *de facto*. Today, it is simply impossible to operate regardless of the global system.

The connections among us even obligate us to be connected emotionally, and not just because of the climate, industry, the global banking system, or education. Today we have to establish good connections with one another, as do countries. Our technological and cultural development, indeed, our whole evolution has come to this state. The inanimate, vegetative, and animate levels of Nature, as well as the human level, have evolved to the point where we are becoming a single entity, seemingly a single person.

This brings up the question: "How do we make these changes in our connections, since without that meaningful connection among us, we won't be able to survive?" Today, genuinely good relations among us are required simply because of humankind's stage of evolution. Without good relations, we won't be able to set up the right laws required for today's economy, industry, and commerce.

Indeed, the world is bewildered and disoriented. We don't know what to do next. It seems as though people have lost contact with each other because now they are required to establish a deeper, more emotional connection, one that's never existed among them. Previously we would either degrade one another or connect to one another for lack of choice. We could even be very close to another person because of common interests, such as industry, trade, education, culture, and healthcare. But people and countries have never been *required* to treat one another kindly.

Today we are required to make emotional efforts in our relations with others because our development necessitates it. We feel that without these relations, we will not be able to continue to exist together in our common "home." If we lived together in the same house because we had no other choice, and each inhabitant had his or her little corner, it would be fine. But today we don't have our own corners. Rather, all of us are roommates, so dependent on one another that without the right attitude toward each other, our lives will be simply horrific.

At our current point, we have no choice but to go for "domestic reconciliation," which is actually "mutual guarantee." We must establish reciprocity in our relationships, a bond where we are all convinced that our lives literally depend on one another. It is like an elite unit in the army, where the life of each soldier depends on the others in the unit. If each of the soldiers doesn't look out for the others, they might all pay with their lives.

There are such systems in Nature, and there are technological systems that exist in mutual dependence. They are called "integral systems" or "analog systems," in which all the parts are interdependent. If any part is removed, the entire machine stops working. It seems that after all the evolution of human society, we, too, have come to such a state of strong connection and complete mutual dependence.

How do we mend ourselves so we can live well and safely? We can do it through "domestic reconciliation" through an outside force. For example, when a couple faces trouble in their relationship, they often turn to a third party, a professional counselor, a therapist, or a friend, who talks to them in order to reconcile them. That person talks to each of the persons in the pair, then to both of them together. That person may ask them questions or provide answers, but in the end he or she makes the couple open up to one another and *communicate*, helping them understand themselves and one another.

Thus, eventually, each party will realize that it is best to compromise and not release everything that he or she holds against the other. In this way, people learn to forgive and accept what they don't like about their partners. To that effect, there is an ancient, yet true maxim, "Love covers all transgressions."

We must understand that our "transgressions" toward others arise because we're all egoists and inconsiderate when it comes to family, our children, in trading, and in every realm of daily life. Yet, we're all made like that by Nature, so we have no choice but to discover what can help us connect to one another.

It is a psychological method that says we need to open up to one another and familiarize ourselves with the nature of the other. We needn't be ashamed of what we are; we must simply acknowledge it and build our connections above all that.

We needn't oppress or admonish anyone for who they are. In truth, we all have our faults, yet we can build connections above them because "Love covers all transgressions." The transgressions are inside each of us, but gradually, out of love, we can stop seeing them.

It's like a mother who believes her child is the best and most beautiful in the world. She cannot find anything wrong with it because she is blinded by love and can see only her child's virtues, not its faults.

But if you asked such a mother about the neighbor's child, she would tell you the exact opposite. She would see the bad parts, not the good ones because she would have no love for the neighbor's child. If she loved that child, too, she would see only its virtues.

Even if we pointed out a negative characteristic or behavior in her child, she would not accept it. She would either justify her child entirely, and say that that behavior is justified, or she would not agree that such a negative attribute even exists in her child. She wouldn't be able to see it. That's the meaning of "Love covers all transgressions."

Therefore, we need to achieve "mutual guarantee" in such a way that we'd begin to learn about the connections among us even before we came closer. The study needs to be from the outset, with the only aim being to build better connections, a bond of love that surpasses our transgressions. That is, right off the bat we will have to start preparing to make concessions because that is the only way we can unite on the emotional level and feel close to one another. Then, the world will certainly be safer and calmer.

In such a state we will not be afraid to let our children out by themselves at night—every stranger will care for them as much as their parents would, and we will care for others the same way. We would have a genuinely good society, one that keeps the law of "mutual guarantee."

Currently, each year we find ourselves in deeper crises. The crises are not only in economics. We have been experiencing unresolved crises for decades, such as the problems of drug abuse, depression, crises in ecology, education, and the disintegration of families.

We must finally understand that the solution to all those problems lies in establishing the right connections among us. Such connections will affect everything in our lives—from family relations to national and international relations.

Therefore, knowing the importance of building the right connections among us is mandatory and dictates that we establish good relationships. This doesn't mean that we sign treaties and contracts with each other, such as peace treaties, trade pacts, and so on. When a couple marries, they make an agreement and sign it, but this is only on paper, not necessarily in their hearts. When they begin to live together, if they haven't formed a bond between them, after some time they cannot sustain the relationship and must break up.

To avoid leading the world into a world war following another outbreak of our egos, we must bring each person to see the connection among us as it is. Each of us must realize how crucial it is that we establish genuine, heartfelt connections among us.

In Nature, everything is beautifully arranged. All the natural resources, all parts of Nature, from the biggest galaxies to the tiniest particles, are connected in a single system. The more science advances, the more we discover the connectedness, the integrality and reciprocity that exist in Nature. We know that if we damage one species, it will have thousands of other repercussions in the world and on our lives.

We must understand that the connectedness also exists in the human society, and today very conspicuously so. Hence, our success depends on building the right connection among us, which is called "mutual guarantee." In that connection, each must feel that he or she depends on everyone, and everyone depends on everyone else.

Accordingly, we must establish new social and international laws. The relations among spouses and kin, work mates, and people in public places must all be based on that rule. Each person, even when alone, must care for our "big family," the family of humanity, for we are all in one place, and we are more connected than kin living in the same apartment.

Such interdependence gives everyone confidence and the sensation of prosperity and abundance. People feel that there are good people around them who want their best, and the whole world becomes family. This way people will no longer be afraid, ashamed, or fear anything. They will feel that "The whole world is mine; I can take a deep breath and feel at home wherever I am—on the street, at home, and anywhere at all."

To create that sense of confidence and security, education is the key. Seeing things as we just described, resolving to relate in this way to others, and working on that resolution within ourselves, require a lot of work. And yet, it is the most important work there is. Now that the whole of humanity is entering this new era, we will have to make this adjustment within ourselves and become not only human, but *humane*.

Being humane means that we are all parts of the human species, which is really a single entity of which we are all parts. We hope that as Integral Education evolves, each of us will be able to see Nature's proofs that we are all one. Scientific research, life itself, and our development all point to our duty to make that correction of connection. If all are convinced to join that education, the new knowledge will help everyone change so we may establish a better world.

Currently, we are at the threshold of this new world. The beauty of it is that as soon as one begins to connect with others, he or she begins to feel the world and life through others. When I love my child, I seemingly experience life along with him: I am with him at school, with his friends, and everywhere he goes. I enjoy what he enjoys and feel what he feels.

Similarly, as soon as you begin to connect to the entire world, you will begin to receive impressions from the entire world. You'll suddenly feel and know what all the people in the world know. In this way, you will be able to expand your life to such a degree that you'll stop living in yourself and will begin to live in everyone else. And at that point you'll be able to touch the eternal point within you, to the extent that you are integrated in everyone else in the system of "mutual guarantee."

The study of the principles of mutual guarantee should be gradual. First we must learn the psychology of individuals, then the psychology of two friends, then the psychology of couples, parent-child relations, attitude toward neighbors, relatives, and all the connections that generate mutual criticism. Out of those we will gradually reach broader circles, even workplaces. Following this we will learn how to expand mutual guarantee on the national level, and finally worldwide.

In other words, there should be gradual progress from close and accessible circles, which we can understand and feel. Then, as we acquire experience and perceptions, it will spread toward broader circles. Finally, we will learn which countries can unite with one another, even which parliaments and rulers can do so. We will imagine these systems in their new form and see how much we are included in them. Thus, we will understand which changes need to occur in the world.

Today it seems that world leaders have become completely incompetent. Because they were never educated for mutual guarantee, which teaches about integral systems, they don't see the world through this lens. They must first absorb the feelings, excitement, understanding, and the methods for achieving mutual guarantee, and finally love.

Mutual concessions must be included in this educational process. Initially, we must aim to establish good relations, understanding that we cannot run away from one another. When we sign any contract or agreement, it has to be clear from the start that we are *not* going to break it. It follows that on all levels, the problem is really only one of education.

There are several ways to reach mutual guarantee. One such way is for people to see and feel, through many examples, how connected and dependent on others they are, and how good it is to be connected properly. People need to see and feel the profits they will gain from it, as well as what they will lose should they choose otherwise. This is one way to convince people to change.

Another way is via group activities. Through questions and answers, games, songs, and films, people will be moved emotionally, experience being for and against bonding and mutual guarantee, and clearly see what each possibility will bring them.

The third way is to use the law, "Habit Becomes Second Nature." If people become accustomed to being considerate toward others and connecting in small groups, they will gradually learn that connection pays off. Then they will be able to pass what they learned to broader circles until they feel toward the whole world as they felt toward their closed circle.

Everything is obtained through the influence and persuasion of the environment, through good examples from others, through films, songs, and anything that affects people. The influence of the environment can make a person do almost anything. It can even "reprogram" people into hating their own children and loving their neighbors' children. The environment is stronger than our own nature because it operates on the human level, while our nature operates on the animate level. Hence, we must use the power of the environment because it can make us act against our innate qualities and completely overturn who we were prior to entering the environment.

In 1951, psychologist Solomon Asch conducted a study that became known as the Asch Conformity Experiment, demonstrating how social pressure affects a person's behavior, views, and beliefs. Using the Line Judgment Task, Asch put a naive participant in a room with seven other people who had agreed in advance what their responses would be when presented with the line task. The naive participant did not know this and was led to believe that the other seven participants were also real participants.

Each person in the room had to state aloud which comparison line (A, B, or C) was most like the target line. The answer was always obvious. The naive participant sat at the end of the row and gave his or her answer last. There were 18 trials in total and the bogus participants gave the wrong answer on 12 trials.

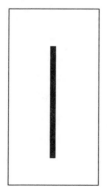 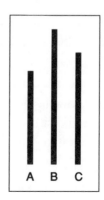

Results: On average, about one third (32%) of the naive participants who were placed in this situation went along and conformed to the clearly incorrect majority. Over the 18 trials, about 75% of the naïve participants conformed at least once and 25% of them never conformed.

Thus, the influence of the environment is the strongest of all the influences, changing our habits and our makeup. It is also how we grew up and what we were taught. You can teach a person anything, and what's been taught is very hard to erase. Therefore, the purpose of the study is to correct that egoistic distortion so that through others, through the environment, people will benefit themselves.

In the end, it is precisely in mutual guarantee that they will find the most guaranteed egoistic gain because they will gain by everyone around them caring for them and seeing to their best. For that to happen, all we need is to make some concessions, but we already pay for everything anyway. In fact, there is no concession here at all because the moment people relate to others well and with love, they will also enjoy the giving.

The idea is not that people will be constantly frustrated, stressed, and feel that they have no choice but to be nice to one another. Rather, we should use external influences on people such as the media to change them so they will naturally act this way. That way they will begin to enjoy their favorable attitude toward others. They will feel that they are in a perfect world because they are being treated well from all sides, and they treat others likewise. Everything should shift from the mode of compulsory to the mode of voluntary.

To summarize, our current crisis is multifaceted, pointing to what is lacking among us—mutual guarantee.

The crisis is not happening because we want the change. Rather, it is mandated by Nature, by our own development. The first step toward it is mutual concessions, followed mutual consideration.

Mutual guarantee is the network that ties us all together. In the 1960s the Club of Rome wrote about it, and in the early 1900s scientists began to talk about us being connected through a concept known as "Noosphere." Since then there have been numerous studies about it.

To spare ourselves and the world further crises, we must learn to install mutual guarantee in all our life systems. For that, we must build an information system that inculcates knowledge, and a system that teaches ethics and behavior, not knowledge. In time, these systems will affect people, groups, the environment, the nation, and all the nations together until we are all educated by the same paradigm— one that teaches us how to live together successfully. We have come to a new era where we *have* to change our relations from self-centered competition to mutual guarantee, and from there to mutual love.

CHAPTER SIX

As Soon as We Feel It

DISCOVERING THE INNER CONNECTION BETWEEN US

W e are in an unprecedented situation. For the first time in history we are experiencing a comprehensive crisis engulfing every realm of life. Many experts in various fields maintain that the root of the crisis is faulty connections among us.

Unlike before, changing a social or economic paradigm will not resolve the crisis all by itself, nor will developing new technologies. Such moves, which always helped us move forward previously, will not help in the current crisis. Today, we understand that even with a technological breakthrough that enables us to develop and produce whatever we want, we will not resolve the crisis, as this is not the heart of the problem.

Instead, we need to examine the direction toward which our desires develop. We naturally follow our desires. It is like a couple who cannot get along and want to divorce. Even the best material conditions will not change how they feel about one another. However, if they loved each other and wanted to be together, they'd be content with a single room. Put differently, today reality demands that we mend our connections first, before we mend anything else.

Children are also drawn only to what they find interesting, good, or pleasurable. People follow their desires, and today we need to examine where our desires are leading us.

We've been evolving through our desires from generation to generation. In the early days of humanity, our desires were quite basic—food, reproduction, and family. Our lives focused around those issues. As technology evolved, we began to take interest in other engagements. We learned to manufacture and sell, to buy products that others produce, and we've developed industry, commerce, and science. The human race began to produce surpluses, causing people to gradually disconnect from the soil as a source of livelihood.

As more time became available for other engagements, we were drawn toward erudition, writing, and culture, and the demand for them grew among all classes. We continued to develop, became politically organized in countries, established industry, and discovered lands. Humankind evolved by constantly wanting more. In the 20th century we even began to reach outer space and dug deeper into the ground and the sea, reaching as high, as far, and as deep as we could.

But then a standstill occurred, as it sometimes happens when we feel that nothing we do interests us, and we just want to leave it all and give up.

In the 1960s a new generation arose. This generation despised everything and began to feel that all these previous engagements were pointless. They were called "flower children" or "hippies." Commentators thought that they were only tired, as it wasn't long after WWII, and the Vietnam War had just begun. Or they thought that perhaps people were simply bored, that they "had it too good," and that was why they rebelled.

Yet, those were not the reasons. It was something deeper. A more developed desire arose in those youths. They didn't want to settle for having a better life; they wanted to know *what life was for*. They resented being reared to fit into their expected "roles" in society, and protested against being turned into "robots" so that someone else would gain riches or political power at their expense.

Our desires are evolving still. Today, matters have come to such a state that there are general despondence and depression. But beyond the despair, we can see that there is a certain direction to Nature's evolution: more and more people are beginning to ponder life's purpose. They cannot settle for just living, partly because life is becoming increasingly difficult, and partly because the evolution of desires prompts their urge to know what life is for.

Today many people receive little pleasure from life, and even less hope. Instead, the prevailing mood is one of, "What can you do? Such is life." Despite the fact that we are living in a generation that really does have everything, more and more people are falling prey to depression.

Yet, what is it that we lack? We can learn any trade we want, we can be artists, we can become musicians, we can have countless hobbies, and we can travel the world. And still, the desire evolving within us doesn't seem to lead us anywhere. We have no wish for anything we've known so far, which is unique to our generation.

Thus, we've now come into a deadlock from which we can escape only if we apply the right response—finding the meaning of life, and finding it precisely in the connections between us. This is hardly the answer we would expect, but the crises around us and the rejection of everything we have in life clearly show that our problems all stem from one source: a lack of positive, solid connections among us.

Let's take medicine as an example. People are losing faith in doctors because, thanks to our intensifying egos, medicine has become a business. Today, without private medicine and expensive health insurance, it is not easy to survive. Medicines have become products, and the pharmaceutical industry is trying to sell as many of them as possible. As a result, we are sent for numerous redundant examinations, some of which are harmful to us and include radiation or injection of toxic materials. Instead of the devoted family doctor we once had, those who treat us now send us from one doctor to the next, as if to avoid taking responsibility, and at the same time, supporting other doctors' incomes.

In short, even if the picture painted here seems extreme, there is no doubt that many of the problems of modern medicine stem from its commercialism. Under such circumstances, it is no surprise that increasing portions of national budgets are being turned toward the health system, with little to show for it in terms of actual public health.

This is just an example of the lack of trust in our society. The ego has spoiled our relationships, and the same is happening in all areas of life—with the authorities, at work, in line at the supermarket, and generally wherever there is human contact. We seem to run up against more and more situations where people seem to be "out to get us," as though they *enjoy* others' pain.

People are now regarding each other as means of profit, ignoring the human being in front of them, and considering only the possible gain or loss connected to that "object." In the financial system, in commerce, and in industry, we keep running up against hurdles because people are considering only their own gain instead of the benefit of *all* parties involved. This is why we need so many regulators to secure our public interests.

Worse yet, organizations spend millions, if not billions, simply to hamper the profits of their competitors, hoping to *make* them fail so they themselves will gain at others' expense.

The lack of good connections among us is hampering the functionality of all our systems. It is especially conspicuous in children's education. There is no coordination among the parties involved in children's education—parents, teachers, and the authorities mandated to educate our children. Every element in the system tries to promote its own interests, and the result is that we are failing to rear the next generation properly.

This sorry state is making people ponder why they should have children in the first place if they will only suffer in such a world. After all, the situation is deteriorating by the day. Personal security is shrinking fast, and there are even predictions that within a few years the world as we know it will come to an end through a nuclear war, natural disasters, lack of food or water or energy, or all the above. In such a state, why have children?

Relationships among parents and children, and parents and grandparents, are also changing. There is no connection among the generations, and family units are simply falling apart.

Also, our attitudes toward our birthplaces have changed significantly. Today we can relocate to another city or another country very easily. If we can overcome the language barrier, we can live anywhere we want. Yet, this only increases the disconnect. There are people who spend their entire lives traveling and don't feel that they belong to any place in particular. Yet, within us is the demand for warmth, for a safe haven, a home. It is our nature to want it.

We can see that if we stay on our current track, we will not be able to solve our problems. The mistrust and lack of goodwill between us are at the core of every crisis. We've always thought that we should think technically—calculate profits, raw materials, and products. We didn't care about the people behind those calculations.

But now this attitude isn't working. We are discovering that we need to instill warmth, care, and *trust* into our relations, or everything will collapse.

Therefore, beyond the "dry" calculations, we have to add a favorable attitude—put some efforts into our relationships, learn to make concessions, and put a little bit of our "selves" into our ties. Without such a change of attitude we won't be able to keep functioning because our desire, the thing that makes us act, wants to be fulfilled and satisfied.

And yet, you cannot put a price tag on fulfillment. I enjoy my son's smile because I love him. I wouldn't sell him for any fortune. Also, I rely on the people close to me to take care of me as much as they can, and you cannot buy such feelings with money.

In other words, from the family's daily life, through the healthcare system, through education, culture, and to economy, trade, and security, it all comes down to the fact that we have lost contact with each other. We are not taught how to create and cultivate connections with others.

In the past, such connections among people were more natural, but today we perceive that connection as a commitment we'd rather avoid. Even when someone treats us well, we feel that this attitude is burdening us. And yet, without love for one another we will simply not be able to live.

Previously, people were more connected to their lands, cities, and countries. They were farmers, patriotic, grounded to the soil and to their countries of origin. Today, these characteristics have become blurred, and when we lose our origins, our homes, which are very important to us, we feel a sense of pointlessness.

It is not a coincidence that the crisis we are now experiencing is encompassing all realms of life. In fact, the crisis began a long time ago as a crisis in people's personal lives, expanded to include family connections, then to education, culture, health, and security, and most recently, the economy. In all the years prior to its eruption in the economy, we didn't pay attention. For years, we didn't mind giving up our emotions. But now we cannot ignore the situation because we're at the end of our rope. If we step back from the financial aspect and look back into our hearts, we will see that if we don't restore trust, we will not continue to exist.

Our society is growing more closed, tighter, and more linked. This is a natural process of development. We can observe it, criticize it, scrutinize it, but it's nonetheless a fact, and you can't argue with reality. Whether we want it or not, it's an inherent process within Nature that simply must take shape.

Therefore, we have no choice but to build ourselves as a society in which people are more connected, warmer toward each other, and treat each other with consideration. It's even written in many ancient sources that we humans must eventually come to love one another.

People who live close to Nature also testify to it. They feel the love that exists in Nature, which runs through the whole of Nature, and they feel Nature's "care" for everything in it. But when we look at Nature from our self-centered viewpoint, it's hard for us to see it.

I once asked famous primatologist and anthropologist, Jane Goodall, who studied the behavior of chimpanzees many years ago, what she felt while she was living among them in the woods, with the apes accepting her as one of them. She said, "Love, this is what I felt existed among them." She also discovered love toward the trees, the forest, the sky, and the earth.

Initially, she was completely detached from Nature, so it was interesting to hear about the process she went through and what she had found. A person who lives in the wild for so long, and has come to the jungle from the urban jungle, slowly discovers that Nature is love.

Can it be that the long process that humanity has been through was intended to develop in us a recognition of the necessity of love between us, so we would open up to love and embrace it? After all, love cannot be forced. We can cause people to behave more politely or more kindly to one another, and we can obtain almost anything with money, but we cannot buy love.

Love is a very special feeling, superior to all other human emotions. We can develop relative trust, which we maintain as long as we need each other. But should a third party come along and offer one of us a better deal or promise greater pleasure, we would lose the trust and mutual support between us. Thus, we are as important to each other as what we might obtain through one another.

We are now in a very special situation. Evolution has brought us to clearly feel that we are dependent on one another and need good connections between us. We need to actually love each other or we won't have the required trust between us to establish a good life.

But it is not by chance that we have come to a point where we are holding "atom bombs" behind our backs. It is with good reason that our lives are filled with cruelty, wickedness, and frustration. This is all happening so we will understand that we have no other choice but to completely shift our relations to the other extreme.

In the middle—between the love and the hate between us—is the crisis signaling that if we don't turn the hatred into love and build genuine trust in one another, we won't be able to survive on earth. Beyond the financial crises, the atom bombs, and all the other inventions, we need to see that we are living in a closed, circular, connected system. It is already so whether we like it or not, but the present system is loaded with arms and hatred. Thus, we have no choice but to transform ourselves. The crisis is showing us that within a connected system we must turn hatred into love, or we will come to a state where we will have nothing to eat.

These are not problems we can ignore, as we might with education. The economic crisis is going to touch us "in the flesh." Many people are already unable to provide themselves or their families with the basic needs of life. And when a country stops assisting its citizens, people take to the streets.

Mutual inconsideration will lead to a state where no country can cope with its problems, even if it is as rich as Germany. Even if there are warehouses packed with gold in the country's treasury, they won't be able to provide decent living conditions to people because of our inconsideration toward each other. Even today, half the world is practically starving while the other half is throwing away enough food to provide for every needy person in the world, with surplus. This is why unless we learn to love each other we simply won't survive.

Why do we have to live in such a world? Why do terrorism, wars, waste of energy, and pollution exist? Are they not all because of our inconsideration toward each other?

We must learn what it means to be considerate and begin to build similar systems in which we will try to establish a more balanced standard of living. Without establishing relations of love among us, we will not succeed in anything. We must achieve complete consideration of each other, understanding each other's needs and seeing to having them satisfied. Otherwise, life on earth as we know it will end.

If the Law of Love is man's general law, how can we implement it? We must set up all the desires within us—however many—in such a way that we do not use them for ourselves, but rather for others. Each of us must be connected with the rest of the world. It does not mean that each of us must know every person in the world, but that each of us will feel that we are all together, that we care for others as we care for ourselves.

How can we change our egoistic nature so drastically? We are living in a special era. Never—in every circumstance, internal and external—has Nature or our own development demanded us to change. We've always gone along with the developing ego, exploiting the world to the best of our abilities. Now, for the first time, we must tend to ourselves and provide ourselves with global and Integral Education that will lead us to becoming considerate of others, to being like good kids in kindergarten. Without such an attitude, our big blue marble will no longer exist.

If we ask sociologists and psychologists, they will say that the proper framework for such an educational process is a group. Therefore, we should set up groups where we can hold discussions, trainings, activities, and exercises by which we will discover the benefits of being together, seeing how much we gain by having considerate people around, and how many beautiful and enjoyable things we can do when we work in collaboration and mutual support.

As we evolved, we began to engage in commerce, industry, and science. But if we reeducate ourselves into growth not on the basis of egoism, but on the basis of mutual consideration and connection, we will be freed from problems and concerns for our provisions, and we'll be able to establish a new industry. This time, however, it will be a very different kind of industry—not one based on technology, but on the *heart*. This will be "spiritual technology."

Until today, we've been developing technology through the ego, which has prompted us to develop. If we tend to our internal development, we will develop a new world, an internal one, full of emotions, insights, thoughts, and new developments and discernments. These will appear within those good relationships between us. When that happens we won't need the Internet or the communication lines we use today. We will connect to one another *emotionally*.

As soon as we include the awareness of our interconnectedness in our already existing ties, we will free ourselves up to experience a very special development, a *qualitative* one. We will begin to feel one another as a mother feels her beloved child.

In that state, it will be as though everyone were emotionally mingled with everyone else. We will begin to feel what is happening within other people, and they will feel what is happening within us. Thus, we'll arrive at mutual consideration and comprehensive and integral connection among us. We will begin to feel what Jane Goodall and many others mean when they say that love is the general law of reality, that love is what exists in Nature.

Sociologists and psychologists explain that through exercises in small groups, we can achieve such profound developments that we will truly feel the inherent forces existing within each of us. By so doing, we will feel the comprehensive love that exists in Nature.

If we improve our relations we will certainly reach more than a successful Common Market. We will find success in every realm of life, a happy life.

Today about a third of states' budgets go toward public health. Yet, only a fraction of it is used to actually benefit citizens. Other large chunks of states' budgets go toward defense, security, and other bureaucratic issues. If we act with mutual consideration we will free up about 90% of the time we spend on things that bring us no benefit whatsoever. We will suddenly feel that it is pointless to work so hard.

Just as the current crisis is forcing us to rethink our attitude toward life, we will have to understand that man must be free, and that we must be more considerate of one anther. Then people will *run* to work out of concern for others. They will build, produce food, and manufacture clothes and other staples, and they will develop the required machinery. However, first they will see that all of us are equally happy. Then, perhaps, we won't need dangerous nuclear energy and other redundant things. In short, things will fall into place according to our consideration of others, the opposite of the current trend.

Karl Marx, whose ideas formed the basis of communism, saw the perversions in human relations from the economic angle. With his calculations, which he presents in his *Das Capital*, he showed that if matters remained as they were, the method would destroy itself. He was right. We may agree or disagree with Marx, but he did see that the ego would exhaust its evolution, and that only at the end of the evolution of the ego we would discover how finite it is, as is happening today.

Therefore, the sooner we perceive that the global and integral world demands us to be considerate, understanding, and to love one another—that this is the general Law of Reality—the sooner we will reach the end of the crisis and the beginning of a good life.

We should begin to move toward it, perhaps initially in small steps, even if just for our children, for the next generation. If we can educate them to be a little more considerate toward each other, they will be happier than we are.

We can already begin to picture the systems that we need to build in order to affect those changes in human society. We need to build new systems, set up groups and train them. Of course, first we must prepare teachers and educators who understand these things. The teachers must first feel them, since without becoming what you teach, you cannot teach others. Through various activities, people will become considerate of each other and find the benefits in this mutuality, both in terms of inner calm, and even in their bank accounts.

People who take to the streets to protest testify that they are happy to be together, to feel that they belong to something, that they have something in common. They feel it when they go out to yell and protest together, true, but is this the right way to go about it? Couldn't we achieve the objectives of the protest by having festivals, giant-size picnics, to which people flock? Why shouldn't we introduce a positive way of life instead? Why should people not feel partnership, consideration, connection, and unity?

The trainings in the course will make us will feel how much there is to gain by uniting. We are going to see how much we gain by being closer to each other, how much safer and healthier the world will be. Bullies won't threaten our children at school, and children won't be exposed to drugs or be afraid when they go out on the street. We will be considerate on the road when driving, so that scores of people aren't killed in road accidents each day. We will stop the arms race and heal the healthcare system. In general, we will build ourselves as a single, warm family, above all the gaps and above all the problems.

And we will do it *along with* our egos. We won't suppress our egos, but will work together with them, just like a family whose members understand that each person is different, unique, and we must be considerate toward everyone.

Love means that I love the other, although he may not be the way I wish him to be. This is how we'll come to have a "round" world, where each complements the other, invokes in the other—through love—the changes he would like to see in the other, so he would love him, thus achieving peace and wholeness. This is the first step toward obtaining that wholeness.

To achieve it, we must establish systems that teach people. Once a person has gone through a gradual change, following participation in the courses in which students comprehend it through exercises, a person comes to *want* society to be more balanced and have a relatively uniform standard of living.

First, we must come to a state where each of us has the basic needs of life. Within five years, we should reach a state where everyone has a roof over his head, sufficient provision of food and clothing, and everything one needs for the household, each according to one's own definition of "household needs."

Provision of necessities will rely on surpluses. If we calculate, we'll find that we have a 90% surplus. When people love each other, they give without feeling that they themselves are losing. Also, if people give up ten percent of their salaries in favor of someone else, in the end, they will not feel it.

The change has to happen at the level of countries on a global scale, and it has to happen through *education*. Education comes first. The change can't happen by force, but by our own volition. The Bolsheviks in Russia tried to impose change, and we saw how it ended. So first, we need education.

Each time we do something for others, we need to show what we've achieved. We have to show wealthy benefactors what the poor receive, and how they contribute to everyone's sense of balance and happiness.

We need to show that through mutual participation we can rid ourselves of surpluses, that we're not producing thousands of redundant medicines just to make someone rich, while sickening and poisoning the rest of humanity. We also need to re-examine our expenses on security and defense, and avoid spending fortunes on the needless purchase of arms.

Nature has brought us into a new era in which we need to mend the egoistic systems we have built. The crisis has reached such a state that if we do not act to resolve it, the population will shrink and we will not be able to sustain the redundant egoistic systems we have built. This is why the world is declining and falling into a crisis. We need to see how our corrupt attitudes are causing all the evil, and how good attitudes reveal treasures, truly a gold mine.

And as far as resolving the global crisis, first we need education. Instead of talking about economic solutions, shortages, and division of surpluses, we need to understand that as part of our evolution as humans, we've come to a point where we have to begin to connect because a network of connections is appearing among us, compelling us to maintain good contacts with one another.

The faulty connections among people are the reason for all the crises—in families, education, culture, and economy. These crises will not calm until we resolve them through heartfelt consideration and mutual trust. Only then will we be able to develop systems that will correct that which needs mending.

In the world, as well as within us, a global, integral form is appearing. There is nowhere to run. It is not by chance that Nature has stopped developing us as it has done thus far.

Before a person discovers the bad, before deciding that there is no choice but to change because he or she is in a life-threatening situation, a person will not come to the new education. We must see that we have no other choice but to reeducate ourselves and build new systems of living.

Psychologists say that to build those systems, we can use the power of the group. Sociologists mention other systems, too, such as politicians, schoolteachers, educators, and sports team coaches. We should be assisted by whatever and whomever we can. We need to build systems that will make people understand why it's necessary to change, as well as how to implement it. These systems will be where people can learn these things.

Nature is pushing us toward a situation where we *have* to determine our next step in evolution. We've always evolved blindly, but now, for the first time, we need to develop on our own. Until today our egos have been pushing us to develop. We rushed to develop anything we could, discovered and developed numerous things while myriad people were selling each other their products. This is how we have evolved.

Now a sudden standstill is happening. It is the first time we have to stop and reflect on where we have arrived, and what has happened. Our children no longer look at us as role models; they're seemingly telling us, "Why did you bring us into this world? Why did you give birth to us?"

We were running forward, but now we've stopped and are wondering where to run to next, and why. Indeed, where has this running brought us, but into a desert of desolation and emptiness?

So first, we need to recognize the situation that has formed as we evolved. We need to recognize it and *understand* it, or we won't reach a state where everyone is considerate of others. In the past, policy was determined by a handful of scientists or politicians, sages, or a king. This has changed. A new law is appearing, which *everyone* will have to keep. This is why we need education.

It is impossible to force people into following this law, or fine or imprison those who don't. We need to instill this law right into our connections with others, into people's hearts. This time it's not about buying or selling to each other; it is a new and special situation.

Today many people are talking about a process that is just beginning, and which is on another level of development. That process is called "the evolution of man." We are building among us a single image, a reciprocal system, a mutual connection called "Man." There cannot be anyone, anywhere in the world, who will not want to partake in it. We have no choice; we *have* to reach everyone because we are all interdependent.

But first, there must be a genuine revolution in children's education in the new generation. That way we'll at least see the new generation beginning a good, balanced life of consideration and safety, a life where no one hits another person, sells children drugs, or lures them into prostitution.

Our children are reflections of us. Because we haven't changed ourselves, we cannot keep our children from behaving differently from us. How can we ask them to behave well when we give them bad examples? This is why our children are rejecting us. They may be worse than us, but they are merely continuing the trend we started. It can't be said that they are bad, but that we are running downhill and our children are running a little ahead of us because they are the next generation.

We have an opportunity for introspection. We can experience all the stages of the inner revolution and shift to a whole new direction. We need to do it because life is committing us to do so, not because some "wise" person thinks so. We need to examine all the scientific data from psychology and sociology, and from our own lives, and see how we can build a new world together.

In a world of loving human relations, an egoistic person will enjoy using the ego in a reversed manner, seeing examples of prosocial behavior and imitating them, thanks to the power of society. Thus, we will learn how to realize ourselves in a prosocial manner, which will be supported by society. This will affect us through reward and punishment and through support from our own kin because we value their appreciation.

We can play with the ego in many ways, according to the environment we build around us. There are four levels of development—still, vegetative, animate, and speaking (human). In accord with those levels, we need to build an environment that contains several levels.

For example, we can influence people through their kin. If my kids look at me and assess how beneficial I am to society, it could really shake me up. We also need to use the influence of neighbors, coworkers, and other acquaintances.

We need to build people an environment that is not inescapable, like a prison. It has to be considerate of our egos because our nature requires it. We need to teach people what they will gain not by suppressing the ego, but by using it correctly so they enjoy using it in favor of society.

If I have children and can use my ego to make a fortune to secure their future, is it bad to use my ego? Our problem is not that we're using our egos; the ego can be a great asset. The only question is *"How* we use it?" If society is compelling us to use it positively, we can expose all of it and use it favorably. If we are using it not so favorably, society should make me rush to fix it. It all depends on the social framework. Man is a result of his environment, which is why we have to act without pressure and oppression.

We all need to take courses on the new world, on human psychology, human relations, parent-child relations, relations between couples, children's education, the structure of society, the history of egoistic development, and study the global and integral systems through the functionality of the human body and the entire universe. We need to be a little more aware of what's happening in the world. However, we need to learn it in a pleasant manner—without tests, but with discussions and mutual consideration, in study groups.

It will not be a class where you come to study and go home at the end of the day. Instead, you will be in a special atmosphere because you need to get to know yourself and the world you live in. It will be similar to the way in which children learn, because we want them to know the world they live in, too, and how they can best use everything around them.

Now we need to give the very same education to ourselves, the "grownup children," because we weren't given it when we were kids. In fact, we're now learning about the "me" and the "world," about how "me and the world" should become "we and the world," and then how "we and the world" become a single, integral "one."

We need to educate people toward such a reality because the general Law of Nature is balance. Accordingly, we must always strive to be in the most comfortable position. Everything moves toward balance. We need to show people that the laws of balance act in physics, chemistry, biology, and zoology. Hence, human society must also be arranged according to that law.

This isn't mysticism; it's science. Using the global crisis, Nature is obliging us to follow that law. To do that, we are turning to experts in various fields, such as scientists and psychologists, for assistance in building our future society.

To summarize, change must begin right now. The problem is that people get used to the bad rather than to the good. My grandfather, for instance, was a very humble man. He had an old mattress with a dent in the middle of it. Over the years, his body took the shape of that dent. When

I offered to buy him a new mattress instead of his lying in a "bowl" he refused and said, "I'm fine. I'm already used to it."

This is *not* a good life; this is habit. People get used to a lot of things; they even get used to fighting with each other, and habit soon becomes second nature. Habits erase any negative feelings and make it ordinary. Habits calm us with their familiarity.

I once spoke to a man who spent 25 years in a labor camp prison in Siberia. When he was released, he didn't want to leave. He had no idea how to cope outside because his entire world was the prison. Next to the prison was a town whose residents were all ex-convicts. Like him, they didn't want to go anywhere, so they settled down in that town for the rest of their lives. The town was in a very desolate place and there was nothing there, but the freed prisoners couldn't imagine how they would cope in the world, while Siberia held everything that was clear and familiar.

As soon as we feel one another, we'll be able to discover the network of connections among us, the internal communication from heart to heart and from brain to brain. Scientists maintain that we are connected in a single field on the human level. Just as there are electric force fields, magnetic force fields, and gravitational force fields, there are other force fields. We know that there is a force field of thoughts, where one can think something and another person will suddenly sense it, or someone will want something, and another person will suddenly want it, too. There are many people who are sensitive and can detect these things.

As we study, we develop our sensitivity toward others so that we begin to feel and understand one another, even without words. We can exit ourselves to feel the whole of humanity as though they were our kin, our friends, as though they move deeper and deeper into our hearts, and we then feel that we have moved deeper and deeper into theirs.

A connection among us is formed, a connection that doesn't require Internet, words, or anything else. Rather, this "heart to heart language" is all we need. It's like lovers who don't speak but simply look into each other's eyes and smile those silly smiles. That feeling, that they are in each other's heart, is all they need.

But here we're talking about more than that. It isn't just a feeling of infatuation. Rather, it is all the wires of the Internet, all the modes of communication, all the commerce, culture, and education beginning to be experienced in our new, "inner technology." We're suddenly discovering through our inner connection a place where we can build a new humanity, a new world full of common emotions and thoughts. And there, within us, within that sensation, we can build a brand new world in its entirety.

These relations will fulfill us instead of music, literature, theatre, or movies. We'll find everything in them, and won't have to make any physical movements to be inspired by the inner forms of our connection. If all forms of art speak of man's impressions, we will feel it in our connections. We will develop technology for our necessities and spend the rest of our time enjoying life.

Indeed, pleasure is an abstract concept. I can enjoy life without producing mountains of concrete and steel around me. The important element is *inner* fulfillment; it is what we live for.

What does a rich person get out of having a ten-digit sum of money in the bank? He or she gets a *feeling*. It's the sensation that counts! If that money were to be stolen but the rich person didn't know about it, he or she would still be feeling great. In other words, we can provide people with so much fulfillment, they won't need anything more but to sustain their physical bodies, while their fulfillment as humans will constantly grow.

Therefore, everything we see testifies to the fact that we must develop by ourselves, build our next step by ourselves toward our own future state. We are building it; we're not being pushed toward it by force. Instead, first we are discovering that we are miserable in our current state, and then we willingly begin to build a better future. However, we will reach that good future only if we understand, recognize, want, and *build* it by ourselves.

The next step is the construction of a happy humanity, in the perfect state, where we are all together, united with the whole of Nature.

CHAPTER SEVEN

Work and Employment in the New World

OUR DAILY SCHEDULES ARE ABOUT TO CHANGE

Today many people are uncertain and anxious about the future. Economists, financiers, and sociologists estimate that soon hundreds of millions worldwide will be out of work. They will have no income and no *prospect* of having one. According to statistics, one in six people in the United States relies on food stamps for provisions. Many millions are receiving other types of aid, either through soup kitchens, clothing donations, Social Security, or all the above.

Yet, not having an income and not having a job are two *different* problems. The first problem, lack of income, occurs when a person is unable to provide for self and family, pay the bills, save money for old age, and provide for the kids in the future. In the absence of income, the pressure mounts and becomes anxiety.

The second problem is unemployment. People who lose their jobs normally seek a new one. But until they find one—a process that could take months and even years—they have a lot of free time which they need to spend in a worthwhile manner. Also, areas where people are unemployed often become crime zones, where prostitution, drugs, and other negative social activities are rampant. The problem is that to mend the situation, society will have to pay far more than if it hired those unemployed people to do some socially useful service.

A person without a job for several years is often unable to keep one later on. Even an educated person may be unable to hold a job because when one is unemployed for a long time, one loses the state of mind of being employed and keeping a job. This involves the ability to commit, to produce worthwhile labor, to be accountable, and to go to work five days a week.

This poses a huge problem that society may be unable to handle. Consequently, frustration and anger will erupt in the form of revolutions and riots when hundreds of millions of people are unable to find work. It will be like a tsunami washing over the entire planet, a social epidemic that breaks out in one country, inciting restlessness, protests, and moves on like a virus from country to country. No one will be immune.

In other words, the problem with dismissing people from their jobs is the idleness and bad habits that develop over time. Today, society can barely eke out enough to pay for the unemployed for a year or maybe two before it leaves the unemployed to find sustenance on their own.

Worse yet, the number of people unable to find work is still relatively small. But if we're talking about millions losing their jobs, this is no longer a financial problem. We are not talking about providing the disenfranchised with staples, since they won't settle for staples. If there are millions of them, they will have power, they will have a say at the polls, and they will have a say in protests. We already have examples of where this trail can lead. It could be far worse than the Arab Spring. In fact, it could be a European Spring or an American Spring.

The problem is that we never taught people the role of work in their lives. We didn't pass on the attitude toward life that one can acquire—that of re-defining the concept of "being out of work." So let's first clarify the concept behind the word, "work."

If we examine history, we see that as we've evolved, we've become increasingly removed from working to obtain life's necessities. Instead, we have moved toward commerce, industry, culture, education, art, law, accountancy, fashion, media—none of which is an area necessary for existence. These are more of an adjunct to our necessities, yet they compose 90% of the occupations in human society!

People in big cities don't work in agriculture. They don't grow farm animals, and they don't work in industries. They make a living by serving one another in various ways that are not necessary for sustenance.

In fact, millions of people in big cities could potentially be out of work and incapable of providing for themselves. They can't produce their own food, and in case of an economic meltdown and mass layoffs, how would we provide for the billions of people living in big cities?

Until approximately 200 years ago, people worked relatively long hours, but there were no machines, no modern technology. Therefore, what people produced was used only for their personal survival. In those days there were few, if any, service providers in trades unnecessary for one's survival.

Subsequently, industry and technology developed, and today a single industrial plant can produce thousands of cars and machines each day. Stores have such abundant food supplies, we needn't prepare anything at home. Using instruments such as the microwave, we can prepare food quickly and effortlessly, unlike the long hours and labor required to prepare it in the past.

By constantly pushing ourselves, we've developed a new, modern way of life. We've developed technology that allows us to create all that we have around us. As a result, along with progress, we've been given abundant free time, and have filled it up with numerous engagements that have nothing to do with necessities, though we might actually consider them as such.

For example, instead of one general practitioner we have hundreds of specialists, thousands of instruments, and thousands of medicines. As a result, we're totally confused. We use numerous advisors, accountants, economists, financiers, and bankers. There's a whole industry of finance, an industry of international trade. In the last 200 years, we've surrounded ourselves with businesses that have no real value or justification.

A good example of a cumbersome, overblown, and largely unnecessary business is the healthcare system. Over the last 50 or 60 years, medicine has become a multi-million-dollar business. There are numerous medical exams, medications, experts, instruments, and vaccines. But alongside these evident improvements, healthcare mechanisms have become bloated and inflated into a business whose goal is to profit off people more than it is to serve them.

A sizeable portion of the national budget goes to healthcare, yet people still have to pay for private health insurance. We've lost trust in physicians because their minds are on their own profits, unlike doctors in the past whose loyalty was given solely to maximizing their patients' health. Today, without private health insurance, one cannot get decent care.

If we eliminated from the healthcare system those elements reflecting ego, profiteering, power, and success, we'd discover that the vast majority of it is redundant.

Today, most doctors specialize in very specific fields of medicine. While this is justifiable in some cases, it would be more valuable if we cleaned up the problems caused by our life values, our jobs, our frustrations, pressures, and the varieties of pollution we create.

It's easy to show that if one lives without the pressure to achieve, but rather works on becoming more social, entering a healthy, happy society, and enjoying positive relationships, the individual's nervous system and the rest of the physical systems will receive healthy support. Then, problems such as pollutants, steroids in our food, and other problems of modern life will cease to exist. When we see these elements as an interdependent, single mechanism, we will see that when the human body is balanced, general healing occurs—in families, in individuals, and in society.

I once watched on TV the graduation night of all the faculties of law in Israel, a country of seven million people. A stadium was filled with the graduates and their relatives. I wondered, Why does society need so many lawyers? Is it because we constantly need to protect ourselves from one another?

Why do we need accountants and the complex taxation system? We wouldn't need such professions if we worked for necessities for ourselves and our families, and spent the rest of the time learning how to create the right society, built on social justice and mutual guarantee.

But the main problem is that we fill our time with jobs intended primarily to satisfy our drives and passions. In the remaining time we just play rather than doing something important, such as occupying ourselves with our *human* aspects. Instead of wasting our time, we should spend it learning a system enabling us to build a just society of mutual guarantee.

If we examine our current way of life, we'll discover that we work ten to twelve hours a day. We rise early, say goodbye to the kids, put them in daycare centers when they're just a few months old, and rush to work, where we spend at least eight hours.

In the evening, we come home, stopping to pick up groceries and the kids. By the time we're home, we have many last-minute things to do like feed the kids, wash them, and put them to bed. We are under constant pressure.

Once the kids are asleep, we can either tie up loose ends we left at work, watch television, or surf the Internet. Thus ends our day. If we have a vacation, it's because our job pays well. Work has become the center of our lives, which is why it's so hard for us to cope without it.

We're *used* to being in a constant rat race, so we fill our time with work. This is why we wonder, "What am I going to do when I retire? I could go mad from having nothing to do." When we take an interest in a person, we find out what that person does for a living, not what he or she is like as a person, and what his or her interests, hobbies, and preferences might be.

The job is, of course, what counts most. One's identity and status are determined by one's place on the job ladder and the money he or she makes. In other words, we don't examine people, but *positions*.

Since the start of the industrial revolution, we seem to have lost the humane in Man. While we have developed industry, commerce, and business, we still feel like slaves to our jobs. The most important thing for us to do is to succeed at work; it's become the focus of our lives.

Put differently, we're born to work, and we prepare ourselves for it during the first decades of our lives. Thanks to medical advances, we may live for ten or twenty years past our work years, but as long as we are strong and healthy, the important thing is work. The only question we need to consider is, "Is this why we were born and why we exist?"

In the beginning of the Industrial Era, Karl Marx said that industrial development could not continue in its current form. He focused on the nature of evolution, which must always end in a crisis. Yet, at that time there was no awareness of the ecological problems that industrialization would bring—the ruin of the planet, the depleting of natural resources such as gas, oil, coal, water, fertile soil, and the problem of nuclear power plants.

Additionally, we've driven Nature's systems out of balance. Clearly, we cannot go on behaving as before. The current crisis demands change.

Our families are also growing up in distorted family structures, with children being away from home all day, and a disconnect between husbands and wives who are busy outside the home most of the day. As a result, we are not evolving as human beings. Our focus is entirely on professions, and any thoughts of development focus only on work, courses, and professional trainings.

Today's crisis summarizes and concludes our development over the past two centuries. Since the time of Marx, many people predicted that this mindset of work-work-work would end in a deadlock. In the 1960s, some people predicted that if humanity continued on its current path, humankind would no longer be able to exist. However, most of us viewed life from a self-centered perspective; we were blind and insensitive. We didn't want to recognize the fact that we were ruining Earth, ourselves, our children, and our futures.

Now that the crisis is here, we have no choice but to transform everything. But in what way should we go about it? First, the crisis will "clean up" all of human society. Like taking a piece of cloth and shaking the dust off, the crisis will clear out all those professions and roles that aren't necessary for human existence. These professions cause Nature's imbalance because they are redundant and only make our lives harder. They also compel us to work longer hours than is needed for basic sustenance. These professions harm both society and the Earth in general.

The crisis will also stop our tendency to value a person's job or working conditions instead of the *actual person*. We will relate to the humane part in those around us, the part that each of us must complement.

The purpose of Creation, as it appears to us through our evolution, is to lead us into a single, integral society, in balance with the whole of Nature. Now we are discovering that this global crisis is compelling us to do just that. Whether we like it or not, in order to put our lives back in order, we have to be connected.

To connect, we need to learn how to rearrange our entire society. As we are gradually being forced out of our jobs, we need to dedicate the time made available by unemployment to learning how to transform ourselves. We must begin to create a mutual, integral connection, and achieve mutual guarantee. We need to change and find the human within us, and make it a vital part of the new, united society.

To establish such a society, we need Integral Education, which will be available to all. We must set up a network that keeps us as busy as before, except that our activities will be divided into two hours of work, and six or seven hours of learning and activities.

During those hours, we will learn, internalize, and change along with others so we can establish this integral society. Then, we will appreciate people as human beings according to their efforts and their success at being humane, not according to their positions or jobs.

This is a massive task, but without achieving it, we won't rise to the next level that Nature has prepared for us, which is being revealed through the current crisis. The crisis is showing us our next degree. It is showing us the flaws within us, compared to the next state. We see that we must put some order into our families, in our children's education, with our spouses, between neighbors, between nations, and then, with the whole of humanity, and in all that we have done in Nature, which we have been only harming until now.

To achieve all this, we must change from within. We must perceive how dependent we are on each other, and draw the right conclusions. Put differently, we need to create ourselves as humans, something we have never done before because we didn't feel it was necessary.

Throughout history, we were worried about making a living and providing for ourselves. Indeed, until approximately 200 years ago, we had to tend to the necessities of life. But in the last two centuries, industry and technology have so developed that we are producing *redundancies*. We have now over-developed our industries. In fact, now is the time to "recognize the bad," the time when we realize that the ego has led us to use our capabilities the wrong way, and is heading us in the wrong direction.

Instead of giving ourselves an additional six or seven hours freed from worrying about necessities, we've filled those hours with redundancies. Now, thanks to the crisis, we're finally realizing that we have to make that time available to build ourselves as human beings.

We, as well as our children, need this education. Until now we've been concerned primarily with our children getting an education that will get them a job. We paid little to no attention to building ourselves as human beings. Instead, we placed emphasis on getting a job and on learning how to manipulate everyone else, so as to excel over others.

Now we need to focus our education on building our children, as well as ourselves, as human beings. When we do, we'll see a good, integral world, all the crises afflicting us today will disappear, and a new world will arise.

The change will be such that we will no longer perceive life as working from dawn to dusk, with two hours in the evening—at best—for seeing the family and running last-minute errands. We need to turn life into something entirely different. We need to build systems in which everyone works only the necessary hours, and spends the rest of the time learning, training, and being educated. In fact, it is time to change our entire social structure. This is the challenge that is now before us.

For the most part, we're currently viewing the global crisis in regard to commerce, industry, and finance. However, we also have problems with Earth's atmosphere, disintegrating families, crises in education, culture, and practically everything else we do. The two major crises affecting us are the financial crisis and the ecological crisis. These crises are threatening our lives: the financial system is causing stress, revolutions, wars, and riots, and the ecological system complements the crisis with food shortages and extreme weather.

Indeed, the cost of natural disasters in 2011 was among the highest ever worldwide. Costs reached 35 billion U.S. dollars, thanks to a significant increase in such events compared to previous years. Today, the price of disasters is on an upward trend. Experts predict that the damage from extreme weather and natural disasters such as tsunamis and earthquakes, tornadoes and hurricanes, will cause tremendous damage, and will affect far more people than before. We can still see the ramifications of the 2011 earthquake and tsunami in Japan.

As it turns out, the ecological aspect is also related to economic balance. It's hard for us to grasp that it is we who are causing Nature's imbalance, and not only by depleting natural resources. Earth's life-supporting environment consists of a very thin crust, under which there is a huge mass of moving magma. The continents are small pieces of land, riding oceans of a sweltering mass. These crusts are all the habitable areas on Earth, yet we are looting our soil of all its minerals, oil, and gas.

Scientists predict that when the polar ice melts due to Earth's warming, the water level in the oceans could rise as much as 20 meters above current levels. Think about how much land will be covered by water, how many people will perish, and imagine the kind of life those remaining will have to lead.

We are facing terrible disasters and our egos are blindfolding us. In fact, if it weren't for the financial crisis, we wouldn't notice anything until the last minute. We'd be in a state of, "Eat, drink, and be merry, for tomorrow we shall die." But the problem is that it isn't happening tomorrow. Even today, we're in danger of violent civil unrest that will render governments and governance helpless.

For this reason, we should begin to educate people, improve the connections between them, and bring them to the state that must begin to exist among us. The crisis is only a symptom of faulty connections, showing us that we cannot continue in the direction we began two centuries ago.

Marx discussed the fact that it is unwise to continue on the path humanity is on because it will end in a crisis. He was against revolutions and said that the change must come through *gradual* development, that people must be developed and educated. He predicted that we would come to a point where there will be no more work, and that people would go out to the streets and riot, as is happening today. This is why he suggested that, besides making technological advances, we have to develop the people.

His successors left what was important, took what was unimportant—changing the governance—and decided that their prime goal was to establish a communist regime. But how could that occur if the populace had no desire for it, and the wealthy wanted it even less? The solution was to make a revolution.

People's perception of communism has been terribly distorted by the people who rose to power following Marx and Engels. Engels more or less understood Marx, but the subsequent rulers of the Soviet Union created a warped perception of the ideology.

As I look at the progress of history, and how it moves in waves of transformation and development of societies and movements, I see how some people rise above others and lead the historic process. This occurs not by their own doing, but from the work of a vast, integral system that leads us all to the simple conclusion that we *have* to learn how to make us similar to that system.

Today we're becoming critical and wish to change the path we've been on for the past two centuries. We have made ourselves freer by using industry and technology, but instead of leisure, we've created constant overtime with which we only ruin our planet and our lives; we have become slaves to our industry.

It is precisely those overtime hours that we need to free up so we can learn how to be *human*. We need to examine life from a new angle, through an integral perception, which is our main goal. This is what man was made for, and this is why we have evolved over all these years.

To summarize, we have a choice between deteriorating into extreme right-wing regimes and a third world war, and Integral Education, which will lead us into balance. Today we're at a crossroads: either we let our egos lead us, or we activate Integral Education according to Nature's law in order to achieve comprehensive balance.

With Integral Education we will change our perception so that we will no longer regard life as slavery to one's job, our source of sustenance. Rather, we should learn to see ourselves as worthy in and of ourselves, and together with our environments, we should begin to build the new humanity and thus attain wholeness.

When we begin to experience the integral system, we will begin to feel Nature's wholeness and perfection, and that sensation will fill and fulfill us. Our society will become a single entity to us, and with excitement, inspiration, common desire, and common thought, we will enter a state where it revives us. We will no longer feel alone because we will be part of a comprehensive system.

CHAPTER EIGHT

Another Form of Development

A CONSTRUCTIVE USE OF THE EGO

We want to see ourselves living in a new generation. At the very least, we want to see our children living in it. We don't want our children growing up in a competitive society where they constantly have to protect themselves from others, where countries are in constant conflict and under the threat of destruction by nuclear arms, which we have made so abundant.

We don't want our children going through the same ordeals as we have, which are still intensifying. We also don't want them to live in a society where it is impossible to walk outside after sunset, where no one knows what will happen in the next minute, or where living conditions are worsening each year.

The divorce rate is rising, and so is the number of people suffering from depression, despair, and stress, which raises the suicide rate. Even the number of drug resistant diseases has increased, as well the number of rapes and other forms of abuse.

There is also an increase in worldwide unemployment, as well as a rise in incidents of school violence and drug and alcohol addictions. Simultaneously, the number of locations of potential conflicts due to food scarcity, security issues, and social unrest and revolutions are rising throughout the world.

Natural disasters are becoming more frequent, and tsunamis, earthquakes, volcanic eruptions, hurricanes, and tornadoes are happening far more often. Technical flaws, such as oil leaks, also cause environmental catastrophes, and each year, such tragedies grow more and more frequent.

We are truly in a perilous situation. People have stopped sensing the dangers not because they aren't there, but because we cannot keep thinking about them, so we prefer to disconnect ourselves from reality and "go with the flow." However, if we stop and think about the kind of world we're leaving for our children, we'll realize that we are not providing them with a good, peaceful, and secure life that offers satisfaction, warmth, and confidence.

Throughout history, we have developed along with our growing egos, which pushed us to grow and to discover new forms of social, political, and economic life. We've developed science and technology, we've done a great many things using our desire to evolve and prosper. But now we've lost our way; we don't know how to properly implement the vast possibilities at our disposal.

Today, humanity is like a group of people lost in the desert, not knowing where to go. World leaders, decision-makers, thinkers, and scientists gather in various assemblies, like the G7, G8, or G20, yet they don't know what to decide. They have no rescue plan for their countries or for the world.

Our egos have been constantly pushing us, but what will happen if we continue to develop as before? If we do, we could end up in mass destruction, hunger, plagues, and climate and ecological catastrophes. Is there another form of development that we might choose?

We know that man develops through the social environment. We are literally products of its influence, so why shouldn't we form an environment that develops us, and through which we will develop ourselves in our chosen direction? Perhaps this is all we need to do in our generation.

There is a good reason why we feel that Nature is no longer pushing us to develop as before. It's as if Nature is waiting. Now we have the knowledge and sensitivity, and perhaps the means by which to arrange society in such a way that, for the first time in history, we will be able to determine our own development.

It could be that, after millennia of compulsory development by Nature, we now have sufficient information, sense, and analytic abilities to develop, by ourselves, an environment that will advance us. Now our only choice is to place ourselves in a good environment and let it shape us well.

If we use the power of the environment properly, we will be able to correct our nature. Instead of being self-centered, we need to learn to use our egos to construct a good environment. Thus far we have been blind as far as seeing where our egos have been pushing us and what they were doing to us, although we can already see that we are not moving in a good direction, toward prosperity, security, and peace of mind.

We need to build a good environment that will turn us into good persons who use our drives and capabilities constructively. Thus, we won't need to build anything new— except for a new environment.

We could build an environment that is similar to the way we would build an environment for children—where each child receives the proper education and the environment is guided by educators who know how to use the children's drives constructively.

Our developments in technology, economy, and commerce allow us to allocate a lot of time and energy to building the new environment. Eighty percent of those fit to work should actually be working on building the environment, and only 10-20 percent of those fit for work should be occupied in what we need to sustain us.

Research indicates that 10% of the world population is naturally inclined toward helping others. They engage in charity organizations, help the poor and sick, work in soup kitchens, and travel to remote places to help desperate people.

Yet, those idealists are too few. Their desire to help others is also born from ego, which prompts them into doing such acts. While they might even be willing to dedicate their lives to the well-being and progression of society, these natural-born "egoistic-altruists" aren't the focus of the new education. Rather, the focus is on the majority—ordinary people who seek only their own benefit. The idea is that everyone will adopt positive transformation so the world will change, and all those forces currently aimed at ruining the world will turn toward Man's benefit.

The only means for inducing such a change is, of course, education. Education relies on a certain measure of learning, the providing of information. We need to set up courses, a virtual environment, culture, theatre, music, movies, music, books, all of which will describe the environment that must be created in the new world.

Although we have yet to actualize these favorable changes, we can educate ourselves by constructing a good environment for adults just as we will do with kids. That is, we will rise to a higher, more mature degree, from which we will build the system that will affect us most positively.

By doing so, people will be "flooded" with myriad good examples that will manifest any way the outside world can affect us, to the point that we will get used to being affected by these examples. Then we will know just how we must behave. We'll have no choice because the environment will affect us to do so, since we already know the power of the influence of the environment on us.

Even if we do this artificially, the examples we receive will still affect us. While these examples will come from different sources, sometimes against our will, they will still work, first unwillingly and then from our own volition. Bit by bit we will accept it because habit becomes second nature. We will be willing to adopt new values for our kids, and for the sake of our own security and a better future. Now, we must begin to get organized toward this new way of life.

All the crises we are going through, all the states surrounding us in everything we do, are actually disclosures of the flaws we still cannot mend in our nature. Therefore, we first need to understand what the "new life" entails so we may imagine it and fantasize about it. The new life is the best possible, even utopian conditions. Therefore, first we must immerse ourselves in that dream.

Clearly, the best and safest situation is for the whole world to be as a single harmonious family that lives in mutual care, where all depend on all, the well-being of everyone depends on the well-being of the entire society, where one is for all and all are for one. Accordingly, each member will work to the best of his or her ability for everyone's sake, just as today we work for our own or our family's sake. In return, each will receive what he or she needs for sustenance, while working for society's well-being.

Granted, people are very different. Human society is diverse, with myriad religions, faiths, and customs. And yet, we must treat everyone with understanding and respect, including each segment and sector in human society. We need to make room for everyone and respect people's engagements and habits. The idea is not to mold people into a single form or erase gaps and enforce a uniform culture for all. Rather, the idea is for everyone to remain as he or she is, and add to our society the good spirit that will exist among us.

Only the kind of education that gradually changes people will prompt us toward great changes in our social structure, political structure, and international relations. The change will lead to an annihilation of international borders and eventually, the annihilation of the states themselves, aiming to create a single, "round," global humanity.

We aren't determining laws and frameworks, except that everything we do must be in favor of the integral humanity. Everything must also be done of our own volition, through the influence of a good environment that offers a sense of belonging and the ability to make concessions and be considerate to the point of loving others. Thus, we will build the future.

We must understand that we need to organize ourselves against the threats that today's life poses—rising costs of living, crises in education, culture, and in everything our children are exposed to in their surroundings. We need to battle drug and alcohol abuse, prostitution, and poor education, so that our children may succeed in life.

We need to "treat" ourselves through the good environment we will build with the help of educators, psychologists, and people who understand how the new society should be built, and how much it can affect us. It is imperative that all of us welcome that environment, and that we and our children want to be influenced by it. We should start building such systems until everyone is under this good influence and begins to change.

Naturally, we need to set up a communication system here, an education system, a system to provide information, and a new system of values. For that, we need numerous professionals from every existing means of influence.

However, we will not be doing it the way the government and media controllers do it, manipulating the people for their own interests by using whatever means are at their disposal. Instead, we will be doing it *along* with everyone and clearly explaining what we're doing. We are building this environmental envelope so it affects us, but with the participation of the masses, all the people, so that *all of us* advance together in perceiving and understanding our self-construction.

Thus, through self-construction, people will rise in their degree of autonomy and will participate in their own education. Everyone will be involved in building the environment that will, in turn, develop them.

If we do all that, there is hope that of a group of people who have lost their way in the desert, we will build our own good future. This will not be a utopian or fantastic future, but a very real one, in which we will develop according to our abilities to be educated and mutually change through the envelope that we are building.

In this reciprocal manner, we will constantly improve this envelope—the environment that we have built—into educating us a little more. And each time we arrive at a new degree of education, we will rebuild and redesign an environment that will continue to influence us with higher discernments and demands.

Thus, we will find ourselves in a constant state of flux, due to self-study and self-recognition, and will extract the best from ourselves and from the current situation, rising ever higher on the ladder of mutuality, benevolence, consideration, and love.

Anyone participating in this process will not simply commence a better and more peaceful life, in which everyone treats him or her favorably. Instead, such a person will reciprocate that approach toward others through the good education, being an active part in the system. In this way the entire system builds and designs itself.

For the first time in history, we aren't evolving through the thrust of the ego. On the contrary, we are evolving through self-education using the environment. We are becoming less egoistic, kinder, and more cooperative. Then the great crisis in humanity—that erupted due to man's lack of integral education over millennia—will be mended, and Man, as the center of Creation, will be at a level that allows him to build a favorable, suitable environment. In this way, Man and the entire world will achieve correction through each other.

The slogans we hear thrown out in protests all over the world from the masses who demand social justice, just division, shared profits, and dignified living and housing for all, are actually saying, "We can do it. Let's build ourselves such a society. Our planet is ready; it has everything; it is up to us how we use it."

Today we see that people have a view, a voice, and power when they connect and demand what they truly need, and when the demands are truly relevant. This is not the case when the demand is for things only a small portion of the people will enjoy, while the rest are left out. Therefore, the hope of having a decent life above the poverty line, a life of security and good education, depends on building the right environment and the right society.

Man is the only creature with an ego, which develops from generation to generation, from year to year, and from day to day. We develop very differently from animals and plants. And as with any natural phenomenon, we should regard it as a manifestation of the good force.

But when Man begins to use the ego in favor of the self, there are grounds for concern and we must prevent this through education. We need to show that in the end, using our egos for ourselves doesn't pay, that the environment will not tolerate this because it harms it, and eventually harms the wrongdoer, too. By so doing, we make our egos the good force within us, a good quality through which we evolve.

If previously we had to toil from dawn to dust to feed our families, raise farm animals, and till the land, today—thanks to the progress generated by our egos—we make machines and scientific technologies that allow us to work two hours a day to provide ourselves with the necessities, including food, clothing, and housing.

Today the world population has crossed the seven billion mark, yet each person can work an hour or two a day to provide for oneself and one's family without living below the poverty line, with each member of the family having all that's needed—provisions, housing, clothing, heating, healthcare, pension, freedom, and education. We can truly make this a reality.

The instrument with which we can aim ourselves favorably or unfavorably is the intention to benefit others. We should build our society with the same intention, where no one uses this instrument for oneself alone, but to benefit others. Only education that provides us with an intention to benefit others and our environment can save us, making each of us aim ourselves correctly in relation to our work and our behavior.

To keep our babies from being hurt, we make sure there are no sharp objects or sharp edges in their surroundings, that their toys aren't fragile or too heavy, and that these playthings are big enough so they can't be swallowed. Put differently, we envelop ourselves with an environment in which babies can develop safely and favorably. When they grow older and know how to use their games properly and safely, we let them have more of them because we know they will not use them in an unsafe manner. This is how they know the limit beyond which the ego is no longer good.

As a society, we need to show them examples that suit their level of development and the level of education they've acquired. Only then can they monitor and direct their egos properly and for everyone's benefit.

We can define today's human beings as egoists who have lost their way and direction in life, who don't know how to build themselves a good and positive life. Today's people have many demands that they don't know how to satisfy. They don't know how to sustain their families and they fear for their children, who are becoming so corrupt and unruly by the day that their parents can't see a good future for them. Today people are losing hope for themselves, for their families, their kin, and for the world. But because people refrain from thinking about it, they are still able to tolerate this life, which often seems worse than death.

Man is broken, ruined, and lost. He is part of a comprehensive crisis on all levels—environmental, personal, social, in Nature, and in the ecology.

Even our accustomed framework is in crisis, meaning the jobs to which we were so dedicated, and our enslavement to our employers, TV, and the media as a whole. This has had adverse effects on us, so today we are finding ourselves with neither work nor direction, and we feel that we have truly been left empty-handed on all fronts. Hence, we are beginning to ask ourselves, "What will happen next?" and we are becoming more open to at least considering a new direction of development.

We need to see how we can achieve security, health, good family life, and proper education for our children. We need to see what needs to be done so that people have work, as well as other fulfillments in life, including hope and a good atmosphere of security.

To achieve all that, we must change ourselves and society—each of us and the connections among us. This can be done through the only free choice we have, the only means by which we can change ourselves and the social environment: the influence of the environment. Thus, we need to build that environment consciously and wisely.

Our current state is one of helplessness, but fortunately, Man is a clever species that can educate itself. There is no question about today's education being improperly directed; however, we can fix it. We need to examine what type of society we can build in order to educate ourselves. There isn't anyone who can come and tell us, "Do this or that; stop fighting; be good." We ourselves must build our environment with wisdom and maturity.

Nature has "deliberately" made us as we are, so we may change and raise ourselves through the environment. If the environment is the only means that affects a person, we need to build the environment so it affects us in the most positive way. In such a state, we are actually educating ourselves. No one will come to educate us; instead, everyone discusses the problem together in hopes of finding the form of bestowal that will change us and build a new environment.

The true educator treats everyone respectfully and trusts people's abilities to recognize what is wrong. The educator also trusts a student's analytical ability, and his or her ability to develop to a level where the whole of Creation is understood. Therefore, no one will come out of the blue and begin to educate humanity as though we were in a giant kindergarten. We are now correcting ourselves and all of humanity in such a way that will correct ourselves henceforth.

For the first time in history, there is a new development by which humanity is building itself. The current crisis is leaving us no other option but to advance by bringing the humane out of each of us. Each person must rise to the level of participation, mutuality, consideration, and mutual guarantee, the level of "Love your friend as yourself." This is called "educating ourselves to reach the humane level." What's more, we must do it with understanding, recognition, and awareness.

At first, we may not be aware of this change, but gradually, through group activities and conversations in which we reach agreements and common understandings, we will realize that we need such an environment. And while we are in a group, we are building such an environment for ourselves.

That is, we will know what we are doing, why we are doing it, and what changes should occur in us. Each of us will be his or her own analyst, and will also serve that role for the others in the group. Each person must become an expert in human nature.

There seems to be a contradiction here because in the beginning we have to treat people as if they don't know anything. Of course, it is not their fault; this was how they were brought up and what drove them into a crisis. And yet, everyone must be treated with respect for their abilities and their potential to change the entire world.

We began by saying that we are like people who have lost their way in the desert. Now we must find our destination—the good life, which we are now scrutinizing. During this scrutiny and after, we will build a world of abundance right in the middle of our desert.

First, we will act in favor of the group, then in favor of our near vicinity, then in favor of the state, and then in favor of the world, according to the pace of our development.

In this way, changes will occur in people, so they see these actions as necessary for our continuation, since there is no other choice. Indeed, either humanity deteriorates into nuclear warfare and global destruction (which could take place even without wars), or we shift to a favorable direction. This is the crossroads at which we are now standing.

The utopian form must be such that ultimately we will all be living at the same level, receiving what we need for complete, decent living while having concern for others. We will all be able to take part in the life of the wholesome society. Man's passions will not be abolished, and there will still be competition, envy, lust, and desires for respect and domination. The ego will remain as it is, but we will find new expressions for it that will work in favor of humanity.

Here is where we must work in an interesting, new way. These are things that can challenge anyone—how to use envy, lust, domination, pursuit of honors, knowledge, and inherent cunningness favorably, rather than to the contrary. This doesn't mean we need to settle for having food, family, housing, security, health, and nothing more. Rather, we can keep raising the standard of living worldwide and still maintain our balance with Nature. In a balanced state we won't suffer from natural catastrophes and we'll be able to thrive and prosper forever. We do not intend for people to live like animals, settling for the minimum. Rather, *everyone* will live *above* the poverty line.

For that, we need new courts in which people are judged according to their appropriate or inappropriate behaviors and actions. In other words, the environment will still be the educating medium, but everyone will know by the environment's reaction toward them if they are behaving properly or not.

If a person's intention is to benefit the environment, that person and the person's family will be rewarded with honors and other benefits. But if a person acts to the contrary, social pressures will influence him or her into changing that behavior. However, this *will not be done by oppression, but only through reproach of friends, family, and social environment.* The objective will be to feel good about oneself through right action.

We need to determine whether people are demanding only what is necessary for a wholesome life, or not. Everyone's needs must be determined and registered according to the individual's character, habits, and circumstances, and a service will provide everyone with what they need according to this information.

There are many things we need to clarify about how we should manage the social environment. Will there be similar systems to those that currently exist, or will we need to establish new ones? We will need to examine every aspect and try to improve what we can.

We are constantly building the environment as an educating element for ourselves. The environment should always be one step better and more advanced than we are now in order to affect us positively. This is how we can elevate ourselves to a more advanced level.

I constantly seek an image that could best teach me how to behave properly. How would that image affect me? How would I hold it before me as an educating image with which I can stay in touch? In fact, this image is me, having reached a higher level.

And because the image is my "better self," I strive to bring my present qualities up to those of the image I have built. There are traits in this image that I imagine, but they are not fantasies. Rater, they are slightly better traits than my own. I build these by examining my current traits and determining which faulty traits I see in myself today. The bad layer that has now appeared to me is what I wish to mend.

Subsequently, I imagine that layer in its opposite form, in the educating image of the environment, since the image of the educator and the image of the environment are the same.

You need to examine how you wish to see yourself if you were to correct your negative traits in relation to others. That is, you would picture yourself at a more advanced level in terms of benevolence and caring for the environment. This is called "the image of the educator" or "the image of the environment," "the image of society." In total, this is called "choosing a better environment each time."

As you become impressed and inspired by that form, you try to raise yourself to those principles and values, each time imagining a better form and trying to be drawn to it. You imagine forms that are better than you, and come to a point where you are willing to advance, except you don't know how. Then, all you need to do is ask the environment to affect you. If you're in a better environment, you will be encouraged to arrive at the form you are imagining.

How do we come to a state where we feel we are bad? We live in a certain social environment, a social circle. That environment consists of others who, like me, are taking part in the Integral Education. Within this social circle I discover where I am at fault and what I need to correct. This is called "recognizing where I'm bad in relation to the social environment." That environment shows me my next degree, and I can see it because I'm in the environment. If I weren't, how would I be able to recognize the bad? We need the environment as a standard by which to measure ourselves.

If I didn't have bad desires, I'd be connected to others, seemingly embracing with them in my inner qualities, in equivalence with them. "Equivalence" means inner bonding to the point of obtaining the perfect form. I'd relate to others in such a way that I'd be willing to embrace them as if there were no differences between us.

Of course, all the above has nothing to do with physical embraces, but with my willingness to treat others as they treat me—well. Recognizing the bad is measured by one's attitude toward others, by how I compare myself to others. There must be a standard, a scale for it, and this is what I detect—their good attitude toward me, opposite my own bad attitude toward them. That gap between them is called, "recognition of the bad."

Through the influence you absorb from the environment, you feel how inferior you are compared to it. The environment's attitude toward you is considered better than your attitude toward it. Because you're at a lower level, you feel it as a flaw in your ego. This prompts you to improve yourself in relation to the environment.

In other words, on the one hand you feel a flaw in the ego, and on the other hand you have no choice but to approach them, resemble them, and equalize with them. Thus, the environment constantly gives you such examples, and you have no choice but to increasingly match yourself to it, just as children learn from their kindergarten teachers.

To tighten the connection with the environment, we need to exert our own efforts. We need to influence one another into growing closer and more connected. Thus, out of our natural connection we will witness changes in everyone.

To summarize, the most important thing is for us to continue examining the overall spirit of our environment, always striving to remain in the direction of bonding, consideration, reciprocity, and love. Then we will change whether we want to or not. Naturally, no one wants to change. We know human nature. But we'll have no choice but to enter a system that will change us against our initial desire—against our egoistic nature.

The environment will not change us in a way that corrupts anything in us. Rather, it will change only how we *use* the ego—from self-centered usage into constructive one—in favor of others, the environment, and humanity. Then, all who are given this education will change and thus build the new world.

CHAPTER NINE

The End of Ego

WHAT HAS CHANGED
IN OUR RELATIONS?

After centuries of scientific development, we are discovering that there are fundamental laws in our world that affect us and the quality of our lives. Our work in this world is to evolve and discover those natural laws in the world around us. As intelligent beings, we are distinguished from the animal kingdom and can test and examine those laws of Nature—what benefits us, what harms us, how to improve our lives, and how to secure a better future.

Man is not an animal who acts by instincts, guided only by its natural drives, dictating its behavior from within. Unlike animals, man has freedom of choice in his actions. But that freedom sometimes yields undesirable results. Humans sometimes harm themselves, while animals do not. Animals don't use drugs or alcohol, or hurt each other unnecessarily. They eat one another, but only to sustain themselves, not because they have an ego or are inclined to harm or dominate others.

In other words, humans have a "surplus desire" that is not subject to Nature's absolute laws. Rather, we can use our will freely—for better or for worse. Our desires go beyond eating, reproducing, and building a nest or a den. We also want to travel, to see the world, to develop science, knowledge, culture, education, and whatever else makes life enjoyable.

For some reason, humans conduct their lives in a worse way than do animals. I sometimes envy cats and dogs because their lives are good and secure, and they seem to have everything they need. Humans are constantly suffering, stressed, competing, and consuming themselves. When we look at others, we envy and hate them, yet we demand respect from them. Throughout history, we've never known how to use our superior human traits. Instead of establishing happy, good lives, we've come to a place of depression and hopelessness.

The life of an individual begins with the father's drop of semen. Nature has prepared for us a safe place in which to develop, a womb that guards us. Once we have grown in the protective shelter of the womb, we are born into this world. We rest in the loving arms of a mother and father who watch over us because we are dependent on them and cannot cope on our own.

Society, too, watches after children and treats them with understanding until they grow up. This is how it's been for generations until recently, when this, too, has been hampered. But until maturity, when we can stand on our own two feet and sustain ourselves, we receive our kin's support and that of the general society, which aids our development.

We are lenient toward children and provide for their needs because you cannot ask them to be independent while they are still developing. Our relationship toward the new generation is instinctively embedded in us by Nature.

Afterwards, when children become adults, they join the circle of life, and society's attitude toward them changes quite abruptly. Nature's laws ascribe accountability, and the family and the environment demand responsibility and reliability. The wrongs we do when we are age ten, which might be treated as mischievous, will be treated very differently when we are twenty and we can be punished for them.

There is an actual inversion in society's attitude toward us. As long as we're juvenile, Nature and the social environment are considerate and kind. But as soon as we grow older, their attitudes toward us change and become seemingly inconsiderate, while we would prefer to continue being treated like children, and not committed to growth. We would like to be excused and treated as nicely as before, but circumstances have changed. Now we are expected to fulfill some roles if we're to be treated well by the environment. The forgiveness we've been accustomed to throughout our childhood and adolescence is gone.

The change in attitude toward us on the part of Nature is extreme. Among animals, the parents guard their young until they are on their feet and can move and get to know their surroundings. Within a few months or up to two years, depending on the species, the young are set free and must provide for their own food, safety, raise their own young, or become part of the pack.

It would seem that it needn't be that way for us because our society is one of intelligent, knowledgeable, and understanding people. We use intelligence to change the world, making it better and more comfortable. So why can't we make a better world for adults? Once we've reached adulthood and began to run our own lives, why can't we build for ourselves good and favorable relations and continue this way? After all, we see that Nature has promoted us through evolution, made sure we'd suffer and change through pressure, punishments, and torments, so we probably *can* learn from Nature's guidance.

Indeed, if we relate to the social environment properly and build together a wholesome society, we will live as before we were born, when we were protected in the womb, and as we do after birth in the "incubators" of family, kindergarten, and school. Why can't we relate to each other in this way and continue in a favorable manner? Also, if it were previously so, what's preventing us from continuing this good, healthy way of life?

If we examine history we will see that previous generations lived in clans, like villages, where everyone cared for everyone else. The men would all hunt together to get food for the clan, and the women would all stay home, prepare the food, and tend to the children. Everyone was looking after everyone else's children. Today you can still find this form of life in different places in the world.

So why didn't we continue to develop in that form, maintaining that good environment on a broader scale using the technology, culture, and education we've developed? What spoiled those relationships? What changed?

What happened is that our egos grew, and as a result, we've drifted apart from one another. We began to look at each other not as brothers, but as competitors, assessing who was worth more and who was worth less. Now we want to dominate others, "buy" them as employees or slaves. We even want to steal what's theirs because we no longer have anything in common with them, such as keeping a household together.

Our egos began to separate us and detach us from that primitive society, that primordial commune, and spoiled things for us. If our egos hadn't grown, and if we'd be growing only in knowledge, things would have been better.

The problem is that the growing ego is the one prompting us to obtain knowledge and discover new things. The thrust of the growing ego to develop us and the desire to receive more and more, are all good. But if that desire had evolved toward obtaining good things not only for ourselves, but for our environment, it would have been better. If we'd known about it in time and tended to it at once, we'd have overcome the ego and it wouldn't have separated us. We'd see to it that all its actions—nurturing the desires within us—would be turned only toward the benefit of the environment.

But is that possible? History proves it's not. Thus far, we have been developing and our egos have grown into a mountain of hatred, envy, lust, pursuit of honors, and a desire to dominate everyone. This is why we are in such a crisis today. We have everything, yet because of our ill attitudes toward each other we cannot establish good laws, we are unhappy, unwell, and insecure. Because of the competition among us, we are destroying Nature and ecology, since we're using our egos to harm others. We cannot control the ego, and as a result, our lives are growing worse.

Nature, which develops us through its laws and through the environment, treats us in two ways. On the one hand, it intensifies our egos. On the other hand, it shows us how the growing ego within us constantly separates us and positions us against one another. It is the cause of everything that's bad, and we're being punished because of it.

But what can I do if I have two opposite forces within me? On the one hand, there is an inclination within me that causes me to feel satisfaction when I benefit myself at the expense of others. On the other hand, in that same inclination, I feel no satisfaction because when I use it, the result is that everything—society, science, education, culture, and personal life—is ruined by that same power of development, namely the ego. The question is, "Can we change how we use our egos? And if we do, how?

Nature is the force that surrounds us and operates on the whole of reality in a uniform manner, following a single law—the law of unification, participation, and love, the Law of Bestowal. This is how Nature operates all its parts on every level—the still, vegetative, animate, and human. This is why there is evolution, which wouldn't be possible if Nature didn't constantly add heat, food, and everything else required for growth.

If we can't find within us the power to restrain the ego, we must find in Nature a force that will allow us to use it in a positive manner. It doesn't mean that we should stop being egoists, because precisely through this motivation we've obtained many things beyond food, clothing, housing, and health. For a third of the day, in our so-called "free time," we can do many things that would be good for everyone.

If the ego has brought us to such excellence in our technological development, we must learn to use it for the best, to harness it and steer it away from hating others and toward loving them. Thus, we will maintain our standard of living, and will continue to develop in every realm of life in this world, family, children's education, culture, health, and everything else.

If we only knew how to use our egoistic nature in favor of the environment and society, we would develop ourselves and our surroundings, and we would do it in a good and favorable manner. We'd think about how to give people the ability to take the *whole* of society into consideration, so they would feel as people felt thousands of years ago when they lived in clans, in small villages, when we were all kin. We will help people come out of the state of not thinking of others.

Long ago, people considered everyone as one entity because the ego still wasn't developed in people. But can people today progress with their egos so they are above them, regarding everyone as related, as family? Can we suddenly find a cure that would make us see the world through an integral perspective, that all are one? How can I regard all seven billion people as parts of me, something I didn't know or feel before?

This would be very different from myself today, when I patronize others. Instead, I would feel that I had to take care of them at least as well as I would care for myself or for my children, whom I care for even before myself. What is the "cure" by which we can mend our relations and our attitudes toward the environment and toward humanity? If we find it, there is no doubt we will be able to continue thriving despite the crisis that is seemingly arresting our development. Now, it's as if we have nowhere to develop; we're at a deadlock, feeling as though we've lost our way in the desert without knowing where to advance.

Therefore, we need to consider where we can derive the strength to use our nature in a positive, rather than negative manner. Currently, we constantly want to bring the whole world under our own governance for our personal benefit. However, it is we who are suffering from this intention, yet we instinctively operate this way. If we inverted our attitudes and thought of the well-being of others and the environment as we think of our own children, instinctively, the world would be filled with love.

Moreover, perhaps we will finally understand that it is we who are ruining our world; corruption is not coming from outside us. Perhaps if we established among us relationships based on kindness, consideration, and unity, we would cause Nature and the environment to become united and considerate, as well.

Recent studies have shown that all parts of Nature are interconnected, that Nature is "round" and integral, and that we are adversely affecting the inanimate, vegetative, and animate levels of Nature. If we establish good relations among us, then not only will our behavior toward Nature and the environment change from the current trend of corruption and ruin, but the quality of our relations will improve, as well.

The relations among us are also based on our mental and intellectual powers, the powers of our desire. These are the greatest natural powers in reality. These forces exist in that same field, passing through our entire world from end to end, and governing all systems—from interstellar to human. Therefore, we may, by balancing our relations, induce greater balance in Nature. Not only will we become balanced, but our entire world will become calmer and more balanced.

Nature teaches us that the only way we may influence people is through the environment, precisely because of our egoistic desire to rule over the environment. In other words, beyond being alive, people depend on the environment, wanting to rule over it and use it for their own benefit and "bend" it so it is under their rule. If we position a person in an environment that presents the opposite—expecting a person to be kind and considerate, or it will reject that person—the person will have to invert the original tendencies to envy, lust, honor, and power to follow society's demand to favor others.

It is precisely that evil inclination within us that demands a connection with the environment, except currently that connection is such that the evil inclination is king. Without revoking that connection, the environment can make us understand that if we want to be great and proud, we must operate kindly, not cruelly. Gradually, because we depend on society, that person will understand that the desire to be in favor of self, to the detriment of society, must be inverted to be in favor of society.

We can see this in the corrupt examples in our world. Take a person who wishes to be elected President. In fact, that person wants to rule, showing everyone that he or she is great, can set new laws, establish a new regime, and create a new government, while being superior to all others. But then the nominee tells everyone the *opposite*: "I will serve your needs better than anyone; I have only your interest in mind; I am your best choice; I will be like a father/mother to you."

This is common behavior in many situations. Our intentions toward the environment might be completely egoistic, but we understand that we must act in the opposite way, so we pretend to do so.

Thus, there is only one way to induce change. If we show people an environment that will educate them toward new values, we will have no problem. An egoistic person who wants to be President, who promises everyone jobs, housing, vacations, healthcare, and security, will be treated in this manner by society. The society will say, "If you want to be the President, first work for us, bring in good results, and then you'll get appreciation. You'll get what you deserve according to the good things you can do for us."

In other words, we're returning to the situation where we cannot complain to anyone. While we are trying to change our lives, we cannot ask anyone to change. We're not pointing a finger at people, demanding them to change. That demand, that whole approach, is very unwise. What we can do is reach every person *indirectly* through the environment, and affect him or her in such a way that that person will receive all he or she needs, without making any effort. That person will grow as if in a greenhouse, with the right temperature and moisture, in ideal conditions, and by playing and acting, that person will grow into the mold of the new society, and will be happy, just as children learn by playing and thus become more understanding grownups.

In other words, it's all up to the influence of the environment on a person. If we're smart, we won't have to think of how each of us should change. Instead, we will create a "theatre," a game of life that is fun to play. We will spend the free time the ego has made available for us on building a good, proper environment for us. With the help of educators, assistants, and teachers, and without any deep contemplation or effort, we will grow like children who grow by playing, achieving the change with ease. All we need to know is how to wisely use that free time and the laws we are learning about, and how to bring ourselves into the proper form.

We didn't do this previously because we didn't know about it. We were too naïve to see the evil in us. We thought our egos were helping us develop, and we didn't regard them as bad. We felt they pushed us ahead, building ourselves families, societies, and countries. But we didn't feel how removed from one another we'd become. We didn't realize the ego would inflict such ruin and harm.

Only in recent years have we begun to realize how desperate we are. Only by building a new environment can we influence ourselves to create "new humans" in an incubator-like environment, or greenhouse. Like a sculptor, this environment will mold us into new beings. Instead of using the power that we have above the animal to be bad humans, we will be good humans.

For that to happen, we will use the power that exists in society, in the environment, in humanity toward a positive direction. Anyone who begins to bond with others will feel that he or she is together with everyone in heart and soul, one mind, seemingly one body. It will be so strong that we will perceive those thoughts and desires roaming in the world, and each of us will seemingly include the whole of humanity within us.

Then we will see how evolution and Nature's impact on us have brought us to a wondrous state where each of us feels the self as the whole. We will come to a state where a person exits the sensation of this brief and limited life, and begins to feel the integral world through the whole of humanity. In this way, we will actualize the primary force of life. The ego, which separates us and elevates us above the animate level, will then raise us to the human level.

As animals, we are different from other animals in that we desire to use the environment either in our favor or to the detriment of the environment. Using the environment for my favor means that I want to receive everything that the human environment has to offer. If I want to use the environment in a crueler manner, meaning to its detriment, then I may exploit others' money through fraud, or invade another country to enslave its people and take its natural resources.

In other words, Man rises above the animal level in two aspects: in regard to the environment, and in regard to human wisdom. On the one hand, the human environment is something that animals don't have. However, Nature has built the human environment for us, tied us to it, and compels us to live in it, if we wish to live in comfort. We could not exist as humans without it. If I were to live in the jungle, I'd descend to the animate level.

Therefore, when we use the environment to its detriment, we eventually end up in a crisis, since we are interdependent, and that dependence causes us to hate each other. Then, everything comes to a halt and life isn't good anymore. It brings no joy, freedom, or warmth. On the contrary, life is so mechanical and intimidating that we prefer the escape of drugs or alcohol, or even try to kill others because we don't know what to do with those around us.

It's a terrible situation, but this is our reality. We're dissatisfied with life, we look at our children's schools and the atmosphere there, and no one is satisfied with what they see. All we can do is tell ourselves that it's the least of all evils.

On the other hand, we have human intelligence, which animals do not. With it, we can criticize the things we encounter and draw conclusions, such as that the source of our bad lives is our attitude toward the environment. If that attitude is turned to good, we will be able to feed the entire world just on the surplus food production we currently discard. The funds we spend on arms would be enough to build a house with a swimming pool for every person in the world! There is also much we can do to preserve the ecology in every area on the planet.

A few years ago people were excited about a new particle accelerator in Switzerland that was trying to discover the Higgs boson particle, which supposedly exceeds the speed of light. Building that accelerator required collecting money over several years, but the amount required to finance that entire project was equal to the amount of money the U.S. army spent in just two weeks in Iraq.

This is just one example of what we could do with money if our attitude toward the environment were different, and we weren't wasting such fortunes on defense and arms. We can see what treasures we have, a gold mine that we are throwing out to sea, and our egos are consuming everything, preventing us from using our resources to have a good life.

If we could examine what we could acquire when the global arms race stops and the waste of over- production ceases, we'd see that five to ten percent of the world population could provide for all of humanity. In other words, the only reason we're over-producing is because of our egos.

Therefore, we needn't think that if we produce only what we need for sustenance we'll be left spending our free time basking in the sun. To maintain the right attitude toward the environment, we will need to partake in *creating* that favorable environment several hours a day. This is why we are being given this "free" time. Every person relieved from caring for self will need to accept everything that the new world and the new relationships entail, and then tend to those new connections. To be liberated from caring for self, we will have to promote our relations with the environment, constantly giving them preference above the inclination of our egos.

We're talking about using known forces of Nature, but people will agree to this only when they have no other choice, when millions of unemployed take to the streets and mothers are afraid to send their kids to school because of violence, drugs, and prostitution. This will be a situation where people are afraid to go out into the streets, and no one will know what will happen tomorrow in regard to personal security and health care.

In such a state, the entire development of culture— which is very important to us as humans—stops. We have to determine that living such a life is not considered a life.

Even today, fewer and fewer people wish to marry or have children. Our own children don't want to exist, and question why we brought them into the world. We're coming to a generation that sees no future, and we cannot live, much less develop without envisioning a future. This is why despair and depression are the most common illnesses worldwide, with antidepressants given even to our pets!

Theoretically, we could have evolved beautifully, as in previous generations when we were developing instinctively as brothers, all together. But we failed because while we were evolving naturally with our egos, we came to a state where only now can we see that the ego is our evil inclination, which harms us. Who among us ever thought that his or her ego was bad?

For instance, when I was a child I loved technology and science, so I studied them at school. I also participated in various courses and later on went to university. When I finished my academic studies, I worked at a research center. My ego was constantly pushing me toward things I thought were good. I wanted to get to know the world. This was a certain type of desire for control, except it was not aimed at forceful domination over others but above it.

At that time I thought I didn't care about humanity; I didn't want to look at all those pathetic little creatures. I wanted to be godlike, to know everything that's happening, to be at the level of the laws, the highest qualities of Nature that govern man. I wanted to understand and absorb everything—the wisdom in Nature, the capabilities of Nature—and not just to be superior on the human level. Although at the time that trait was not that evident to me, in retrospect I realize that it was stemming from a desire to control.

I remember how I related to humanity and to everything on Earth. I didn't only want to absorb our planet, I wanted to be at a level where I absorbed the entire universe. While that approach is egoistic, in those days it drove me forward toward development. Only later did I realize that if development is not in favor of humanity, it is bad.

Actually, there are several degrees of "bad." I could be bestowing upon humanity because I had no other choice, or because I wanted to receive greater rewards for myself. Alternatively, it could be that I simply loved humanity. Although I think I will benefit from giving, I begin to understand that doing so is good even if it doesn't immediately reward me. There is a special force within that trait that warms my heart and broadens my sensations so I only enjoy loving others, not what I might receive from them in return.

All of a sudden, great hollows emerge in our feelings and awareness that we are currently unaware of. But gradually, through cause and effect, we open up more and more qualities that were latent and that are now evolving. Although these are trivial things that we already use, those qualities are already in us, but previously we had no recognition of evil, so we couldn't use them to treat ourselves.

We need to understand that it is precisely the growing ego that pushes us to obtain wisdom. This is how it promotes us. Although it's ego, it's not the evil inclination. There are two levels to the ego. One level is where I want to fill myself with knowledge, a good feeling, food, sex, family. It's as if I were alone in the world, hurting no one, just like any other organism that satisfies itself. Another level of the ego is where there is an evil inclination, when I want to fill myself with wealth, honors, and knowledge, things I can obtain only by exploiting the environment and exploiting others.

Wealth, honor, and knowledge are degrees above the animate level. These are human desires, which I use to satisfy the human part in me. They derive from the ego and stem from my desire to satisfy myself as much as possible. This is the part called "evil inclination," when I want to satisfy myself by oppressing others.

And there is also another part that manifests when I use others as they use me, in a good way, as in a family, as with loved ones. In a family, I use those I love and they use me for mutual pleasure, mutual benefit and fulfillment, so we are happy and content. This is the bonding part: we could be friends, a couple, or just anyone. Because it involves using others, it's also considered ego, inclination, desire, but it is not bad because it doesn't intend to harm others.

Only if I intend to obtain pleasure by force is it considered evil inclination because I want to enjoy without considering others, or while harming others.

There is a broad range of relations here. I could be taking pleasure regardless of others, or I could be deriving pleasure specifically from hurting others. But all and all, my desire to enjoy the suffering I cause others—or the fact that I have no regard for another and don't care whether or not another suffers—is called "evil."

Let's assume that I committed bank fraud and managed to steal one dollar from every customer, then got away with it and received millions. I might enjoy the fact that I became rich, but I might also enjoy the fact that I degraded others by managing to steal from them.

These are just part of a broad range of attitudes I may have toward the environment, beginning with being inconsiderate and ending with my enjoying the suffering of others. If I am simply inconsiderate, I let others work for me and treat others like the machines I operate. I receive what I need as if it were 200 years ago, when workers were treated as slaves. If I also take into consideration the capabilities of others, I try to use others as much as possible, meaning I take their personalities, knowledge, and skills into consideration. Today, our evil inclination has so evolved that we as humanity enjoy harming others.

These selfish pleasures are signs that we have reached the most advanced level of egoism. In our development, everyone is at a certain level and my ego enjoys considering how much I am superior to you, how I can exploit you.

It's no longer enough to be rich if no one but my banker knows about it. I enjoy only if everyone sees my fancy car, yacht, that I own companies and control people. Also, I enjoy oppressing others because money alone doesn't satisfy me anymore. Rather, I measure myself in relation to others.

All the above is considered "using others to the detriment of others" because I want to be above them. This is what's causing today's prevailing sense of dissatisfaction and rising suicide rate in the wealthier countries. Nothing is enough for us anymore; we're at a dead end, and we can't receive any pleasures anymore.

Yet, the ego is also developing us. It's bringing us into a state where we don't know where to go. It's brought us to a point where we don't enjoy even the desire to be superior to others. And if I can no longer enjoy superiority over others, I have nowhere to develop and nothing to live for, because being richer and more powerful won't give me anything, so why should I bother if it doesn't please me anymore?

Today, Man has lost his motivation to develop, the foundation, the engine of development. He has nothing more propelling him to continue. He doesn't care if he has more or less. He is indifferent about the future altogether. This is a projection of our lack of desire, this helplessness within us. Previously, we wanted to be rich, strong, and wise. Today we want nothing. In fact, we don't even want to continue the species; we wonder why on earth we should have children.

Everyone is in this general confusion. The situation is very complicated, multilayered. The solution is only in our relation to the environment, and its relation to us. If we establish good relations among us, proper ones, we will be able to create a glorious life and will receive new energies, unlike now when we are powerless and have nothing and nowhere to continue.

Until today each of us developed individually, linearly, as though on a straight line from the beginning of time up to this day. Our desire evolved in both quantity and quality, and has brought us achievements. But suddenly there is a stop, no reason to continue. We've come here running and have stopped midway because we have no reason to keep running. We've lost our way in the middle of the desert. It's as though we're in space.

The individual motivation is out, which is why we're immersed in the despair that started some fifty years ago and has inflicted crises in every area—education, culture, and our personal lives. In fact, it is these crises that have caused the stoppage. This motivation will not be renewed, for we have reached the end and have nothing to live for, as physicians who prescribe antidepressants will testify. Statistically, the suicide rate is about one million a year worldwide, a 60% increase over the last 50 years or so.

Now we want to save the patient called "humanity" before it dies. The situation is critical, but it is not hopeless. We can correct it by using the additional power that will move humanity forward. It is a force that does not come from within humans, because we have nowhere from which to draw further desires to live. Instead, only when people begin to connect with others will they find additional powers.

We can see how the patient called "humanity" receives additional powers and comes out of the depression, helplessness, and deadlock. We can see how it acquires its life from its surroundings and discovers that the environment is actually itself, meaning that we are all one. In other words, by uniting we bring back to ourselves parts that are actually ours, but that we didn't feel as such.

It's like a woman who becomes a grandmother—it gives her a new life. She loves her grandchildren more than she loved her own children because now it is the only pleasure she can have in life. To her, the grandchild is literally a cure.

To summarize, our current state is such that if we don't acquire from the environment additional desires from which we will feel great additional pleasures, we will not only end up in despair and depression, but in terrorism and world wars. We will be helpless, hopeless, and won't understand why we are in such a world where it's better to be dead than alive. We will conduct ourselves according to the maxim, "Eat, drink, and be merry, for tomorrow we shall die."

We will experience eruptions and riots just so we can ignore the question, "What is life for?" Even now we can feel the question, but it's still in miniature proportions. People seek peace and quiet in many ways, but can't find any. Later, this will result in eruptions that will lead to wars.

We may be in despair because we cannot find a cure to our situation, but a cure is present. The cure is bonding and uniting. Only by uniting with Nature and with others will each of us receive new energies, support, and warmth. And within the new desire we'll receive from the environment, we will receive new fulfillment.

When we connect to everyone, we will discover within the environmental fulfillment that will raise us to the human level. We will begin to feel our lives above the animal level. We will feel Nature's perfection and eternity, and the relative calm that surrounds us now. We will also recognize the bad that has already been revealed allows us to mend the situation successfully.

CHAPTER TEN

Make the World Prosper Again

BALANCING MAN'S GOOD AND EVIL

During our lives, we go through a process of evolution. We don't see the end of the process in the beginning so we don't understand the need for each of the steps. What is clear, though, is that everything we go through in life seems to us either corrupt or redundant. We're uncomfortable with our character and habits, and most of the time we're unhappy with ourselves and those around us.

We can compare the evolutionary process we're going through to the ripening of an apple. Initially, it is small, hard, and sour. But as it ripens, it absorbs water, minerals, essential gases such as CO_2, and sunlight. Gradually, it grows and ripens. We don't see the need for every stage in the process but in the end we have a beautiful and tasty fruit, the opposite of its sour beginning and ripening.

Like the apple, we are going through a purposeful process, except we can't see it. We don't understand the need for the stages we're going through, or what the whole process is for. We end our lives without understanding that we are moving toward a good situation in which everyone is wise, kind, and good-hearted.

Unlike apples or other plants or animals, people advance from generation to generation. Our next generation is always more evolved than its predecessor. For this reason we cannot look at life from the perspective of a single generation. The evolution of humanity over millennia is like the maturing of a person from the beginning through the fulfillment of his or her destiny, to that person's ideal state.

It is how we evolve. This is why there is a maxim that "you don't show a fool a job half done." The difference between a wise person and a fool is that the wise one sees the future. The wise one knows the end and can therefore justify the process we are going through. But we are fools; we cannot see the end of the work, so it is difficult for us to justify the situations we're experiencing along the way.

True, the process is a long, hard and painful one. We advance by blows, mistakes, trouble, and all kinds of problems, yet we are somehow advancing. But in the current state, we're at a crossroads, or worse yet, a deadlock. It's as if we've lost our way, we're lost in the desert, and we haven't a clue as to where we should go. Again, we need to learn from Nature, of which we are part. Nature is drawn toward balance, and balance with Nature means having the same qualities as Nature.

Since we're in the midst of the evolutionary process, we need to discover the general force of Nature, learn to what is it drawn, what it "wants," and what it sustains in us. If we do, we'll be able to see that we're evolving positively and that this is the way to achieve recognition of the bad, the ego within us. Then, we will understand how bitter a life we're making for ourselves and for others.

We learn that when we wish to succeed through the environment, to exploit everyone and become powerful, wealthy, and dominating, it backfires on us and acts to our detriment. We can see it just by looking at the kind of society we've built, the kind of humanity we have become. Humanity possesses great wisdom and wealth, so why have we arrived at a state we didn't plan to reach?

What is the reason for the emergence of all the evil? Why do we keep making mistakes and draw the wrong conclusions about why we're unhappy? We keep chasing goals that we think will make us happy once we achieve them, then we run to another when the last one has failed us, again hoping that the new one will make us happy. But in the end, it always ends in disappointment, if not in tragedies such as wars or plagues.

If we look at ourselves compared to Nature's other levels of still, vegetative, and animate, we will see that the whole of Nature evolves very slowly. This is because evolution on those levels occurs only by fulfilling natural drives, following instructions from within. For example, if we examine the behavior of a horse, a dog, or a cat, we will see that they act according to their nature. This is why they don't make mistakes. They have their inner laws, by which they exist.

Conversely, humans constantly err. These mistakes should make us evolve intellectually. Yet, although our intellect evolves from generation to generation as we acquire knowledge, an awareness of the world, Nature, and ourselves, we are badly misusing our intellect.

Early scholars such as Aristotle and Plato talked about using the intellect properly or improperly. They laid the foundations of modern science and argued that knowledge must not be given to just anyone, but only to people who know how to use it in favor of humanity. Thus, through this knowledge people will develop good relations toward others.

Knowledge was intended to make life better for humanity. But when knowledge enters the public domain, it actually harms humanity because the ego makes people misuse it, to their own and others' detriment. And then the bad backfires and ends up ruining the environment, sending humanity to make weapons and other needless things.

We see that today, through science and knowledge and our immense capabilities, we've come to a state where we have abundance, which we are using to ruin and spoil. We are in a comprehensive crisis in every realm of life and at every level of the population. Even science itself is in crisis. Education, family, human relations, relations between spouses and between parents and children, healthcare, culture, and the media are all in crisis. There is a chasm between where we could have been, and where we are.

We've been misusing our capabilities for generations. Over the millennia of evolution, we've come to a point where there are people who use science to support various forms of governance over people, to develop arms and needless medicines, which they sell at great profit. Today, science is serving man in ways that man doesn't need, and scientists are selling their inventions only for profit. A decent scientist is one who loves science and acquires knowledge out of love, not in order to sell it.

However, we've already recognized, to some degree, the bad in our development. It seems that we can still develop favorably. We do some harm, turn back, and quickly return to the good. Then we do more harm, then again return to the good. All we need is to activate our sense of recognition of the bad so we may see our mistakes and correct them right away, without plunging into the bad. It's like a little child being given something to dismantle so he can fix it, and thus learn to do it right. We are the same.

All we need is to change our approach and understand that our lives are built in such a way that evil is a must. We must first recognize our egos as bad and use our capabilities above the animate level at the human level, capabilities for which we are called, "speaking," "human." If we use those traits correctly, constantly checking which is correct and which is not, out of such scrutiny we can move from the bad to the good. We will see progress that always occurs through joint action of two opposite forces, like the systems in our bodies that work by contraction and expansion, such as the respiratory system or the cardiovascular system.

It is the same as systems in an engine that operate by sucking and ejecting, or the wheel of a bicycle, where two opposite forces operate on it—one forward moving and one moving backward—causing it to advance.

In fact, in every evolution there are always two opposite forces working in harmony and complementing one another. Therefore, we needn't give up anything we have in our world, because we had to evolve as we have. What is now missing is the activation of our sense of criticism so we can see what is happening and how we can wisely critique all that's been done. Thus, we learn how to advance through corrections henceforth. When we do, all the bad will turn into a means that supports the good.

In this way, we'll be using both the bad and the good for advancing, and then there will be no bad or good, but two auxiliary forces assisting us. All of a sudden, we'll begin to understand that our egoistic nature is good, that through it we've actually developed our ability to scrutinize and correct ourselves.

Therefore, we need to understand that we've been given a good and favorable development, and the addition we receive from the wisdom opposite the ruinous ego (those two forces within us) can help us advance. If we work this way, we can understand that our free choice is right between those two forces. On the one hand, we have the apparent bad force, and on the other hand, the intellectual, good force to help us, since we humans appreciate and respect wisdom.

In between the bad nature and the wise intellect we can find the right, positive way. It is a way that's good for Nature and for us, for all the still, vegetative, and animate. Thus, we will achieve harmony with all forms of life and with Nature as a whole.

Ultimately, the suffering we're going through is really an invitation to activate our free choice and correctly use the balance between the two forces at our disposal. There is no doubt that the whole world needs to understand and use that great force of the intellect in this way, in order to rein in our egos and use them correctly, not to destroy the ego.

There are various techniques and belief systems claiming that the ego is bad and should be neutralized. We need to understand that there is no such thing as "bad" in Nature. There is only the ability to use what exists in Nature positively. If we do not use it positively, it becomes negative. Therefore, all we need to learn is how to use our intellect.

We need to develop the know-how and the method, a program for using the good and the bad properly, to create good life out of the two. We needn't look at what we have right now, as it is said, "Don't show a fool a job half done." In other words, we mustn't be as fools, looking at the process while it's happening and complaining. Instead, we need to see everything as goal-oriented and understand that every stage must be as it is, and that we're advancing toward the good goal. We need to see that the goal is right around the corner, that we are nearing it with each step, approaching a corrected life and a good future.

We mustn't mistreat, demand, complain, criticize, disrespect, or disdain Nature, ourselves, or others. We need to understand that we are all going through the same stages, the same process, and we should help one another reciprocally. This is what people who are lost in the desert need. They will not get to the oasis without each other's help. That mutual correction and mutual assistance are the keys that will lead us toward the good goal.

To establish mutual help, and through it the goal, we first need to understand how we are built. We need to understand that in each of us are three kinds of desires. The first is physical desires, which we call "animate" because they also exist in animals, which follow those desires instinctively. These are the desires to maintain ourselves as best as we can, to keep ourselves clean, healthy, well fed, rested, and provide everything else the body needs.

The second kind of desires is egoistic desires, through which we develop above the animate level. Within us humans are also desires for domination, lust, and honor, and in these desires we want to be superior to others. These desires belong solely to the human species. Animals don't have them. They might eat one another, but not because they want to harm, rule, or govern one another. They act this way only to feed themselves.

This is why a lion hunting a zebra isn't doing any deliberate harm to the zebra; it's simply following Nature's instructions within it. There is no animosity between the species; it is just how Nature works. We, too, behave that way toward animals. We don't hate the cows, chickens, or the fish we eat. We simply eat them because we have to, and we try to do it in as humane way as possible.

It is only toward humans that we use the ego. We look at the neighbor's lawn or the neighbor's car, kids, salary, etc., and measure our achievements in life compared to theirs. There are statistics that prove that people would be happier to make $50,000 a year if it were above the average income in their neighborhood than $100,000 a year if it were below the average income in their neighborhood.

We value ourselves in comparison to others. That is, we appreciate things not in relation to us, but in relation to others. This kind of desires is called "human desires" because animals don't have them. They don't mind what other animals have; they only need to satiate themselves. Human desires, however, are all bad.

A third kind of desires, which are also exclusively human, are above the two previous kinds. This is the desire for knowledge, for wisdom. It is the desire to know what I'm living for, how Nature works, what is happening around me, and how things are connected. In other words, it is a love for the wisdom in Nature, for knowledge, for the study of Nature.

We are in a bubble called "Nature" and we receive from it. We are seemingly in a sphere, peeling it layer by layer. Each layer that I peel I examine, and the laws I discover are called "Science." In the future, I'll discover more laws, which already exist today but I'm not wise enough to see them, to discover them. The more I learn, the more laws I will discover that exist in Nature.

It follows that all people are combinations of the three types of desire—the animate desire, the human desire, and the desire for knowledge. What changes from person to person is the combination of those desires. One may have more of the desire for knowledge, another will want to be superior to others in wealth or status, and a third will settle for football and beer on the couch. Everyone is built differently and there is nothing good or bad about it. Everyone has his or her own nature. The three types of desire exist in everyone, but each person is more inclined toward one than toward the others. Each person finds his or her place in the environment according to the desire within, and advances accordingly.

The most common desire is the one for bodily needs. The evidence of that is that those who wish to achieve power and dominion, and rise above the human society, are few. In other words, if I'm immersed primarily in my physical desires, I use what I have around me to satisfy the degree of my physical needs. If my desires belong to the human level then I want to rise above everyone and dominate them, be superior to them, and be stronger, smarter, and more successful.

If I'm inclined to science then I want to be above the animate desires, as well as above the speaking desires. These are desires to understand, connect to Nature, and see why things are built as they are. I want to learn philosophy and science, and I don't care if I have more or fewer possessions than others. I can eat very little and hardly maintain any contact with people, but it's important for me to connect to what is above and beyond, to the causality of the universe.

There are different people in the human society, and each finds his or her own engagement, builds a family, an environment, and a society according to one's own desires.

Smart people, who use science properly, know Nature and know that there is a process and a plan to it. We still don't know the rules of the process, but we know that one exists. We are still not sure where it is leading, and can only guess that the process is leading us toward balance, such as the balance that exists on all levels of Nature. At the end of the day, we, too, have to achieve balance.

Balance with Nature can be expressed in temperature, wind, storms, and volcanic eruptions. Everything happens in order to eventually yield balance. Nature acts to balance itself and Man, as part of Nature, must also balance himself.

Because there are good and bad forces within us, to prevent them from erupting, we were given science. Through the knowledge we've acquired, we can achieve balance between those forces within us. We can use the bad force and the good force of the intellect to balance them and progress in harmony.

We must balance the force of the intellect with the force of the bad within us. As a human being, I have desires at the still level, namely the materials from which my body is made. I also have desires of the vegetative level—the things that grow in me, such as hair, nails, and bones. Then there are desires of the animate within me. These are the rest of the parts of my body. I also have an intellect, which is a desire above the animate level, and I have the negative force within me, my ego. These are the parts of which we are comprised.

There is nothing to correct in the desires of the still, vegetative, and animate levels. The problem is in our relations with each other. There is where we corrupt our lives, since we have an evil nature, ego, although we tend to tell ourselves that we aren't bad. Others are bad, humanity is bad, or human nature is bad, but not me, personally.

Concern should not be only for my progress, because I am an animal, living in the animate level, and must achieve balanced consumption. Rather, the *whole world* needs to reach balance at the *human level*, meaning that we will all be equal, just as in a family. This is the situation to which we should aspire in the human society, on the human level of knowledge. Thus, we will reach the perfect state, like a ripened apple.

Therefore, there is much important work for us to do. There is no greater or more worthy challenge than the one before us, but through this knowledge we will be able to carry it out to the benefit of the whole of humanity.

Man has vast potential, but while we can act to improve our lives, we aren't doing it. We are detained by our egoistic nature because we want to use all our powers, all our skills and capabilities to raise ourselves above others. In consequence, everyone's competing with everyone else, each of us trying to lift ourselves up while ruining the rest. This evil inclination is not letting us lead the good life we should.

There are other scrutinies we need to make regarding the good inclination and the evil one. For example, how can we picture ourselves living with the good inclination? Doing so means that we all have to be the same. Is it possible that we can be like everyone else? What will we enjoy? If we're all the same and there is no less or more, then we have nothing to live for, and won't feel we're alive. All our activity is aimed at getting more than others possess. Subconsciously, we constantly compare ourselves to others, and that comparison gives us reason to live and pushes us to achieve. We can see it in sports and at work. We *have* to measure ourselves compared to others; it is how we measure how much our lives are worth.

This brings up some big questions: With what will we satisfy ourselves? Does Nature wish to turn us into robots? What does it mean that we are all "kin?" If we're all kin, it means that everyone's equal, everyone has the same amount. But then I won't feel there is something to live for. Is there another goal that I cannot see in my current state?

A person always wishes to realize one's potential. For one person, it may be science; for another, it may be writing, photography, or education. But in the end, a person wishes to excel over others. That need is what pushes us to develop. If we all become balanced and equal because we feel there is a crisis and realize this is the way to resolve it, how will we satisfy the need to feel superior?

In the future, we will settle for two hours of work per day to provide for our needs. But if we all work two hours a day and don't wish to have more than others, and if everyone is equal and settles for necessities, how will we satisfy our desire to excel? Currently, we work at least six hours a day to gain more than others. If those six hours are freed up, we could go mad from too much freedom. Did Nature set it up this way?

Here is where we discover Nature's other side, the side where we use the ego in the opposite manner. That is, the ego is constantly growing, but not so we will be superior to others. Rather, it is so each of us will rise above his or her *own* ego in order to balance with, and be equal to, others. In this way, we derive satisfaction from tightening our bonds with others because the more our egos grow, the more we can bestow upon others and bring them into greater bonding and balance. We will *enjoy* having stronger connections to them.

The more we connect to them through our corrected egos, the more we will enjoy because we'll have a new desire from which to feel pleasure—the collective desire, which we have connected to ourselves by becoming connected. The type of satisfaction we will derive from that desire is called "mutual love." In this way, we can achieve a far higher fulfillment than the one we have today when we manage to excel over others. Therefore, only the correct use of all the elements within us will allow us to reach abundance.

Proper use of all the elements means that within us, we create a balance between the intellect and the evil inclination, the ego. Using our intellect and science, we understand that we have no choice—either we use science with our evil inclinations to produce weapons, or we use the intellect above the evil inclination, and then "straighten" it out to connect to others positively. In that case the intellect will rule over the evil inclination. This is how we achieve abundance and a good, secure life of mutual guarantee.

Balance is not with evil. Rather, balance is in using the evil to be balanced with the human society, with Nature. When I use the evil inclination, I only turn it into good, but I still use the desire in its entirety.

However, in this evil, I want the opposite—to use it for the best. We see that growth, proper development in all the forms of Nature, is always through balance between two forces: the positive force and the negative force. The combination of the two is what yields abundance, so how can I balance the negative force, my ego, which is ruining my life? I have to have something equal to it, and this is my intellect. Therefore, above the physical and human desires, there is a science by which I can balance the human part of me.

Every person possesses an intellectual ability to cope with one's ego. My intellect should be like a driver of a car called "ego," so that with my intellect, I will "drive" my ego to the right development. What is the right development? It is a state where all of us are equal, connected, kin.

The intellect can direct me to such a state, in which I am considered "human," operating with my intellect rather than through my erupting ego. When the ego erupts, using the intellect can lead to all kinds of "creative" breakthroughs, such as the atom bomb. As previously mentioned, Aristotle and Plato determined that knowledge is only for those who wish to control their inclinations.

Because we didn't heed their warnings, the current situation is a dire one. Thus far, we have been following the ego, and supported it with all of our science. Now we must reflect and begin to develop to the contrary, through reason. We must recognize the bad, like a wise man who sees the future. We will see where we need to reach, decide the nature of the good state that we should set as our goal, and then move toward it.

When we do so, we will discover that the evil inclination is "help made against us." It only *appears* to work against the goal, while actually providing us with fuel and energy, stimulating us to develop in a positive direction. We can turn the evil inclination into a good inclination through science and knowledge, and through our examination of what is bad and what is good.

Therefore, using the ego properly or improperly is all the free choice we have.

There is no bad force or good force in Nature; it depends on how we use each force in Nature. For example, 100,000 years ago we were kin--living in the jungle, sharing everything, and all was good. No one thought himself either superior or inferior to others. Then the ego began to develop in us, and alongside it, the intellect began to develop, and it was used to serve the ego. If one person saw himself as more successful than others, he took more of everything for himself, detached himself from the clan, built himself a nice house, and married several women.

In other words, through the egoistic drives that began to awaken in us, some began to consider themselves superior to others, and with their intellect and abilities, began to dominate others until they had nothing to eat. The "superior" person would feed them, and in return for the food, turn them into slaves. The others agreed in order to avoid starvation, and thus became owned by their master. Afterward, the master would build a small army of slaves, conquer some of his neighbors' territories, and become a king.

Even today, we use personal intellect and knowledge to direct situations and manipulate people into rising above them. This is what everyone does, wherever we can. Even people who were once victims of the system have become experts in their own professions and have advanced. Everyone advances, and then others advance atop them. This is how human society evolved.

In other words, everyone uses their intellect to obtain their desires, whether to dominate others or to excel over them. The intellect is the ego's servant, and the ego is the boss.

This is how it was until the arrival of Plato and Aristotle. At that time, the intellect and science began to develop more extensively. It was a special period, during which mathematics and geometry developed.

Then, a problem arose: To watch the stars, scientists needed telescopes, and telescopes cost a lot of money. Where would scientists get the money? They needed rich peoples' money, but scientists had nothing to sell but their knowledge, so they did, in order to build telescopes or other equipment. As a result, science became corrupted.

As scientists built telescopes, the rich who bought the knowledge used it to see enemies coming from afar. With the ability to see them approaching came the ability to defeat them because now the rich man had an edge—he could see the enemy before the enemy could see him. This is one example of how scientific wisdom was used for selfish purposes.

In other words, science became the servant of man's evil inclination, serving it however it was needed. Afterward, rulers took the scientists, kept them under their dominion, and threatened to kill them if they didn't provide them with knowledge.

In other cases, scientists established universities and taught. Thus, science began to serve man in every possible way. We can see that to this day, the majority of science, knowledge, and the money being poured into science are aimed at developing arms and defense.

But in Integral Education, it should be the opposite: science should direct the bad into good. Through our intellect, we've come to a point where we don't need to work so many hours a day for our livelihood. Indeed, the crisis itself is causing this to happen, doing us this "service" by creating unemployment. Now we need to examine and criticize ourselves, our nature, and our way of life. We need to learn how we use our egos negatively and try to invert this into a positive use.

There is a maxim that says, "Who is wise? He who sees the future." That is, the wise sees in advance the expected result, and thus avoids suffering. A wise person is one who sees others, and knows why it is worthwhile to move toward benefiting others. We develop science in order to know how to stop deadly illnesses. The question now is, "How can we picture the process so we can see that if the situation continues on its current course, we will be lost?"

Indeed, how can we mend ourselves? Which medicine should we take in order to achieve a peaceful life?

That same science, that same development, should now bring us the understanding, the sensation, the examples of everything that's happening to us, and the direction in which we are developing. Science should bring this to us in a way we can feel, and help us establish this as the public view. It should be created so strongly that we will not want to use our evil inclination against others. Instead, we will understand that any benefit to others is our benefit.

When I feel that another person wants my good, I will see how I can "buy" the other, what I can give so as to make the other's attitude toward me favorable. By doing so, I turn that other into a good person who doesn't harm me. In this way we will not deteriorate to a state where we are indifferent, hateful, and repelling one another. We will not reach the point of avoiding living with one another, or starting a family, or having kids—the future toward which we are currently moving.

In the past we lived as families. We lived in a single house with brothers and sisters, relatives, and grandparents, and everything was fine. Today we don't want anyone around us. People hardly tolerate themselves to the point of taking drugs to avoid feeling themselves. We're moving in a very clear direction. With all the violence, rape, and bullying today, soon we won't be able to go out of our homes and feel safe.

Children are already frightened to go to school each morning because there are bullies and drug dealers there, but they have no choice, they have to go there. If this continues, they will feel they are surrounded by a hostile world. This is not a place we want to be in, so we need to start fixing the world right now.

Each of us must determine how we will use each force in Nature. The desire to have more than others isn't negative in itself. It's negative only if we want to oppress others.

There are two possible states: I may look at another person and not be envious, but rather learn from that other person's good qualities. This is good envy. But if I look at the other and think, "Why do I need to work so hard to have what he has? It would be best if he didn't have anything. If I ruin what he has, I'll have nothing to be jealous of and I'll feel much better."

So the whole issue is about how we use each desire or inclination. The inclination itself is neither good nor bad, just as with envy. There is good envy and there is bad envy. Good envy promotes me because I want to grow. Bad envy directs me to destroy the other. Either good envy makes me want everyone to be rich so I will have something to aspire to, or bad envy will make me want everyone else to be as poor as I am.

The test is simple: do I want others' favor or their harm? There is also an intermediary state. If it's not for another or against another, but only in my favor, it is at least progress from wishing another harm.

However, my looking at another and wanting the same thing for myself doesn't bring us into balance with humanity or Nature. In the end, during the evolutionary process, Nature doesn't require that we learn from one another and be constantly immersed in competition. Rather, Nature requires that we provide ourselves with a balanced, decent material life, and beyond that, evolve as humans with mutual connections. In this way, everyone will be satisfied through their connections with others. We should fill ourselves with love, not with fancy, pricey, newer toys. We are in a crisis because we're not doing so.

Lately, we feel that there is nowhere to evolve. We're tired of looking at others; it doesn't give us any pleasure. The economy and technology are unable to keep up with the pace. Earth doesn't have enough resources to maintain this endless competition. We can therefore see that Nature's plan is not for us to develop towards what appeared to be "happiness." The situation in the process we are undergoing requires that we recognize that there is nowhere else to go.

If a person sees a beautiful car in the neighbor's driveway, it's seemingly neither good nor bad. However, it could turn to bad if a person who was content riding a horse and carriage saw that his neighbor now had a shiny car. The coachman would begin to feel deprived and deficient. He knows he needs to work much harder to afford that car. This puts into his mind thoughts of envy and vengeance. The problem is not the self-assessments we make in relation to others. Rather, it is that Nature doesn't allow us to continue the competition.

I'm all for competitions that make us happy, competitions in which I want to be as giving to society as you. This is constructive competition, in balance with Nature, and toward the same goal. When I look at another and learn from the other, I do it through envy. The other person is great, and I am small; the other is succeeding, and I am not.

About what am I jealous? If I'm jealous of things that bring balance, peace to me and to the world, promoting me and the world toward obtaining balance, toward becoming a "ripe apple," it is good envy and good competition. We need to encourage it, reward it with prizes, and present such people to the media for all to see the good example. But if by competition we're not advancing toward good things, but sink into problems and trouble, moving away from the goal, this is bad envy and bad competition. Everything is measured in relation to the final goal because we have no choice but to reach that same balanced mode we see in Nature. By looking at the balance and harmony in Nature, we understand what we need to resemble and the reasons for what is happening to us.

Competition is rooted within us. Man is a social being, and hence a competitive one. Competition is neither a good inclination nor a bad one; it depends on the person using it. It was said, "Envy, lust, and honor lead one out of the world." If I want to advance from my current state and be more beneficial to myself, to the environment, and to the world, I need to use envy, lust, and honor in such a way that my intellect directs me to use them correctly.

We can use all our inclinations positively or negatively. My intellect needs to direct me toward using them positively. This is why we were given intellect. An example of good competition is when two people go to a gym together. They "pull" one another, and because they envy each other's looks, they train harder. This is considered good envy. It's possible that one of them will enjoy the other being less fit and well built, but in the end it cannot be said that the process itself is bad, although competition is involved in it.

When one compares oneself to another, it is a competition. However, there is also competition for the purpose of development. While it is ego-driven, envy, lust, and honor urge one to improve because they increase our desire to be like another. However, the competition is aimed at development. We may also be in a competition that makes me feel bad when I look at the other person because I can't achieve what he or she can. I would not want to see this kind of example because it's not in my favor; it's to my detriment.

Good competition is one that enhances both of us, where we are tied together and cannot succeed without each other. Let's say that two people start a business together. One brings in the money, and the other brings in the knowledge. Without the investor, the knowledgeable one wouldn't be able to succeed, so it's good that they're together. However, partnership can be a source of envy, even hatred. In other words, in many cases there can be a thought, "How great it would be if I were without you," even if the partners are dependent on each other.

There is only one kind of competition where both are dependent on each other, but are not opposite one another—a competition to become one. It is a competition where we measure how much we love each other, when there is nothing between us that we purchased or manufactured. We both want the same result, and thus we're not divided. Neither of us aspires to be superior to the other. There is only one, and that one comes from our mingling in one another, from bonding in all the qualities with which we complement one another. None of us can be alone or acquire that sense of complementing each other in any other way except from mutual love, or at least mutual guarantee as a preparation for mutual love.

Any other solution that doesn't lead us into being one, out of mutual guarantee, will eventually lead to exposure of the ego between us, and to separation. The competition where we become one is the only solution. According to this approach, when we engage in bonding in order to reveal love, even if now we are competing and are still in envy, lust, and honor—meaning in hate and love—it all complements one another. Love is the result of the bonding itself. For that, everyone needs to correct him or herself in relation to the connection with others. After that, the love in the bonding among us will appear.

We have a lot of work to do with the intellect. We are balancing our corporeal lives into a single line, where each receives what the body needs for its sustenance, and beyond that, on the human level, we are sorting out all the evil within us. Above that degree, in the superior degree in us, we develop all our science, knowledge, and intellect in order to provide for our physical needs and in order to turn the evil inclination that constantly appears in us into a good inclination with the help of science, until we achieve love.

To summarize, there is nothing to correct in desires of the still, vegetative, and animate levels. The problem is in our relationships with others. There is where I corrupt my life because I have a bad Nature, or ego. Everyone agrees that this is so. Therefore, the correction of the evil inclination is Man's destiny. We have a lot of work to do in correcting the evil inclination, though it may seem to us that it is simple. Life was given to us and we've evolved as we have to fulfill our physical needs for only a small part of the day. We must dedicate the lion's share of our time to correcting the evil inclination, to reaching the good inclination. By doing so, we will discover Nature's perfection.

CHAPTER ELEVEN

From the Love of Man to the Love of Nature

HOW TO RISE TO THE SPEAKING LEVEL

Man is the only being who changes during life and constantly develops. The process of development that humans go through is mandatory simply because the ego keeps growing during our lives and from generation to generation. We see this in ourselves as well as in others. Each generation is different from the preceding one. Everything changes—culture, political structures, education, characters, human relations in general, and family relations in particular. Unlike humans, animals maintain the same pace, the same style, and the same framework all the time.

A short while after birth, an animal is equipped with all it needs to survive. Within a short time, it knows how to watch out for itself. Conversely, the process by which a human learns takes many years and involves absorbing information from one's environment. Only after many years does one learn how to take care of oneself.

During life we learn, develop, change, and are constantly affected by different desires. We are drawn to one thing and then to another. During life, we change professions, family, place of residence, and areas of interest. Humans behave very unpredictably because new desires constantly arise in us. We cannot know what will happen the next minute, much less in a few years' time.

Within us there is also the animate level. This is the basic level at which we tend to our bodies with food, sex, and family, and relate to our bodies as "animals" would, in a rational and balanced manner. Despite that, there is much that we do with our bodies that is redundant. Some of the things we do are good, but when we overdo them they become harmful. In ancient times, physicians maintained that over-consumption of good things is more harmful than consuming a small amount of harmful things.

Therefore, on the physical level, to sustain our family and society, we need to bring our consumption needs into balance. That said, a reasonable level of consumption does *not* mean that we should limit ourselves to the point of regretting it and suffering. Rather, it is only meant for us to find a good, healthy boundary.

Yet, unlike animals, within us is the speaking degree, above the animate. We should clear the rest of the time we have, once we have taken care of our necessities, and build ourselves as humans. We need to develop the part in us that is above the animal level.

In a sense, we belong to both worlds—the animal kingdom and the human kingdom, which we call "the speaking" degree. The speaking within us grows by connecting to others. There is a lot of work to do in these connections with others. In fact, we need to create from our present selves a human being that has not yet been born. And yet, there is only one thing we need to do in order to achieve it: correct ourselves.

Each of us is born in the animate level as a living organism that has just come out of its mother, weighing about seven pounds. When we raise a baby, we first attend to its physical level, making sure he or she eats and drinks sufficiently and stays healthy. We treat the baby as a living body. Afterward, it grows and we follow its reactions to noises and sounds, light and darkness. It begins to move its body, first with involuntary movements and then with voluntary ones. We buy our babies toys and thus help them develop. If we didn't interfere in the process as humans, producing everything for them, they wouldn't grow as humans but as animals. The human in us develops only through the education we receive.

The problem is that our education is entirely egoistic, urging us to exploit the world. We understand that to keep ourselves safe, it's best not to hurt others, to avoid taking from them, and to be lenient. Then, we will be treated well. We teach children that if they behave kindly to others, others will reciprocate. This is why, as part of our education, we direct children to stay on good terms with everyone so they don't arouse hostility toward them. We understand this and therefore educate them to act this way.

And yet, our egos are affected by the media, Internet, TV, and the general environment. These shower us with bad examples. While we don't want them, they affect us against our will, and we teach our children how to trick others in order to survive in this world. We send them to martial arts classes or to study law so they know how to protect themselves in this world. And yet, we see that although we evolve from generation to generation, as well as through our own lives, we are still on bad terms and have bad relations with each other. Each of us builds his or her own happiness, wealth, joy, and success in life by, at least partially, hurting others.

Therefore, because of all that we've been through in this generation and in previous ones, we have reached a state of crisis in our development. We possess lethal weapons, we've depleted the planet of almost all its resources, we're adversely affecting Nature, ecology, and climate, and we are ruining ourselves and the human society. Even outer space near Earth is full of space junk because of obsolete satellites. But most of all, we are dissatisfied with life. There is general despair throughout the world, an acute crisis in education and learning systems, and numerous other problems we've already mentioned.

In the end, we are approaching a decision that we have no choice but to change ourselves. Put differently, all our work, individually, generally, socially, and globally, should be to re-educate ourselves. From relationships of hatred, repulsion, pride, envy, honor, and domination that exist among us today, we need to shift into relationships of consideration, mutual guarantee, and love. These are not just lofty words. We simply have no choice; it is how Nature is directing us. Our development is pushing us into the necessity to establish good relations.

Our parents brought us up to be kind, respectful to others, and considerate so we would have many friends. They explained to whom we should be close and from whom to stay away because they wanted us to choose a good environment. In the same way, we need to educate ourselves because the current situation is becoming life-threatening. Therefore, the only correction we need to make is to build human beings out of ourselves. We need to give our bodies what they need to a rational and balanced degree, and we need to build the human, speaking level of ourselves above the physical life, above our animate level.

In the previous century we busied ourselves developing international relations, international trade, and international culture and tourism. People travel from country to country for their pleasure, yet still encounter very unpleasant situations. If we wish to continue to develop, we must unite.

For example, why not create a common market, not just in Europe, but embracing the whole world? We can see that our egos are pushing us toward it, yet it's also stopping us from establishing proper connections between us, connections of consideration and mutual understanding.

In Europe, too, despite the closeness and the interdependence formed by the establishment of the Common Market, people and countries are still in conflict. Although borders have been dissolved and the coins united, something still prevents them from moving forward. Europe could have been a superpower, like the United States, Russia, or China, but instead it's aging and weakening because the states of the European Union cannot unite into a single power. They cannot rise above that weakness even for an egoistic benefit because of the cultural, educational, and historic chasms between them, which make it impossible for them to transcend past hostilities.

Is it possible to bridge those gaps? It will be, when the canopy of love is spread over our heads. Other than that, everything will remain as it was. The method by which we rise above the ego leaves the differences in culture, education, and even politics as they were.

Every person will live with his or her own culture, education, and religion, yet will treat others kindly. For example, in a family where each does something else— one is a doctor, another is an engineer, and another is into philosophy, all will agree that they belong to the same family and complement one another. In other words, because everyone is so different in views, behavior, and way of life, without a unifying force (the family) tying them together beyond their differences, they would never have met.

Can we do the same so we may have a good life, without wars and destruction, so we may stop the tsunamis, hurricanes, volcanic eruptions, and the collapse of the economic system? It is said that a person will give anything for his life. We are already in a life-threatening situation and we need to understand that we already have a method that is more meaningful to us than all of science. All of science and all our interests in life are measured by our ability to improve our lives. If we have a way to bond that can save us from destroying ourselves, that method is certainly superior to any other science, and we need to look into it very seriously.

The method of Integral Education will save us from all the bad things that are happening. It will not only neutralize the dangers on humanity's path, such as wars, global economic collapse, and hunger. Rather, Integral Education will keep us from harm, lift us toward a good life, and make us feel life on a whole new level. Through our mended relations we will uncover what is called "human," the "speaking level." This is the degree at which we are in touch with Nature's deepest realm, the engine that operates the entire process of our evolution, the thought, the greatest force in Nature.

In this way we develop an ability to feel Nature, feel its eternity and wholeness. When we discover it, we become mingled, filled, sustained by that method. This is what the integral correction gives us, the method of Integral Education.

This is why this wisdom is above all other wisdoms, above all the sciences that humanity has created. The results it yields show that nothing comes close to it. When we understand the importance of Integral Education, it'll be naturally important to us to actualize it on ourselves. However, it is important to pass it on to others because to the extent that we affect others and others affect us, we set an example to one another of mutual bestowal through positive stimulation and pressure, thus we advance.

This is why it is important not only to learn how to treat each other nicely, but also to pass on that positive attitude and serve as a good example to each other. Just as our parents were our examples of how we should relate to life, each of us should educate others.

No one is superior or inferior in this system of education. Rather, one person simply learns from another. This is why we constantly need to show responsibility by giving an example not just to kids, but also to friends and to those older than us, or at a higher social status. Each of us should feel like a guide to others, and that feeling should make us behave very responsibly, to the degree that we will stick to that behavior because the fate of humanity depends on our actions toward others.

These are not just nice words; it is how our nature works. We are affected by each other whether we like it or not, even subconsciously. Even if I have very little respect for a person, I'm still affected by him or her.

Considering that Nature demands that we behave that way toward people, we need to take Integral Education very seriously and understand that humanity is waiting for this education. People need this form of education and will welcome it if we give it to them softly and lovingly, just as we welcomed education from our parents when we were children. These recollections exist in everyone; everyone wants to be treated kindly; everyone needs it.

We need to grow this way, just as we needed parents to treat us lovingly when we were infants, because even now, we don't understand the world around us. But because we need to build a great and beautiful world, once we have felt our parents' love, we begin to feel love from our friends, who are also receiving the right upbringing, and then we feel love in school and with friends, in university, at work, and in society in general.

In other words, we gradually move to broader, bigger "hands"—those of the whole of humanity. We constantly experience consideration and love, just as we received when we were children. We will continue feeling it throughout our lives until we feel that general love as Nature's superior law. In this way, we feel the harmony that exists in the entire system.

Building similar systems among us means building the right envelope or environment for educating people. When we build such people, we are really building only the human, the speaking level, above the animate level that presently exists among us.

Therefore, with a good attitude, consideration, mutuality, and giving, we maintain two modes of behavior: good behavior toward people on the human level, and good behavior on the level of the whole of Nature, in relation to the general law of Nature, which operates in mutual giving and love. Out of this general force, Nature builds the entire process that we are in.

In this way, we are encouraged and reinforced, and we gain twice: by being in a good human society, and by being in balance with Nature. Every once in awhile, we could err with an unbalanced attitude. For example, if we relate in a balanced manner only toward Nature, such as Greenpeace, which cares *only* for Nature and animals, it isn't really helping them preserve Nature. Without proper *human* relations, we won't be able to preserve Nature. The two areas are interdependent. After all, when a person becomes good, he becomes good in *every way*. Such a person will also preserve the still, vegetative, and animate, using them only for necessities, and then Nature will return to balance. Each section we damaged will then be rejuvenated and will reappear, and the whole world will return to balance.

We need to take Nature and human relations into account, and educate humans first. From loving Man, we will come to love the whole of Nature. This is the direction in which we need to go. Even when relating to humans, we need to understand that in the end we have to achieve balance with the general law of Nature, with the general process, and with our entire evolution. It's a process, and we need to come to love people and then obtain the general love that exists in Nature.

The correction we need to make above the animate level, at the speaking level, is built as a process in the human part of me. It is not in the animal part of my body, although I execute it through the body because my body is my tool. The attitude, connection, and the actions toward others—favorably or unfavorably, as before—are enacted through contemplation, speech, and action.

First comes "thought," which precedes "speech" and "action." This is the first thing that I need to devise. It arises from an internal calculation, from the self, and the influence of the environment, society, and my educators. We must design the thought, and then bring it into speech. Speaking is "just talk," unless it is first expressed as action, and then it's valid.

"Speech" means that we need to convince ourselves—through internal speaking, for we constantly talk to ourselves, as well as to others—how we should change and in which direction. We need to decide how much we need change and to what degree we must go through this process of achieving benevolence and encompassing love.

"Action" means that during the hours when I'm free from tending to my body's necessities, I will be studying the Integral Education, or will already be circulating and activating the integral approach toward others. This will bring all people to a decent, uniform standard of living above the poverty line. It will also lead to just division, so no one is deprived in relation to others.

In other words, first comes the thought, then the speech, and finally the act. These must be aimed toward building a new and balanced society where everyone is on an integral level, in an analogous, uniform system.

In thought, I promote myself through the influence of the environment, by constantly wanting to be influenced by a stronger and more united environment. Then, I arrange that thought within me and carry it out by speaking and convincing as I provide others with information. Finally comes the action, when I actively give to others by educating, teaching, and raising the standard of living of the whole world to a state where no one is hungry or deficient of life's necessities. This is basically our work.

In this way we will achieve balance with Nature. The whole time, we need to stress that our goal is to achieve balance among us, and through this balance we will balance with all of Nature. Through the process, we will form a round, complete system.

By doing all this, we will end our evolutionary process, when the whole of our evolution since the beginning of life on this planet finally achieves balance and completion. Scientists say that the world as we know it could soon come to an end. But when we say that it is about to end, we're not referring to a physical end, but to an end to our ego-driven evolution. If we achieve complete balance and harmony with Nature, there won't be any pressures on us by Nature, and we will live in perfection.

Let's hope that at least we'll be able to start feeling that state on ourselves, and thus we'll be able to pass it on to our children and grandchildren. It's in our hands.

We need to understand that this development, which includes persuasion, scrutiny, and correction of our egoism into altruism, where we are considerate and love one another, can happen even in our generation. It all depends on our willingness to change.

Because our desire depends entirely on the environment, we must work together, rather than try to persuade ourselves by ourselves, which will never work. Instead, we should build together an environment that will affect us, and thus we will all change. This is why we must build a good environment for all of us, convincing us and speeding our desire to change and connect in mutual guarantee. As we change, we will increase the intensity of the environment's impact on us to make our change quick and lasting.

The evolution of the still, vegetative, and animate degrees in man took millions of years because they evolved through the ego, which needs to grow in man. We are not responsible for this. Rather, we evolved this way because the ego was naturally growing and as a result, we acted on it more and more.

But now the force and pace of evolution are in our hands because everything depends on the environment. Now we're artificially building an environment, and the more advanced we can build it, the more it will affect us and be great in our eyes—expansive and full of impact. Therefore, we have to use every means at our disposal, including professionals such as sociologists, psychologists, and artists. This coalition will help affect us as intensely and effectively as possible, giving us a happy life together while in this generation. We will finally know, and be happy with what we are leaving for posterity.

We can divide our desires into two: personal or individual desires, and human or social desires. For ourselves, we need to limit our desires to what is required for our existence. This happens during the correction. We also need to develop our social desires with which we relate to others. This is done in consideration of the circles around us, beginning with the closest circle—friends—then broader circles. Ultimately, we will develop ourselves through the influence of the environment, and bring a good, considerate, responsible attitude to everyone, with mutual guarantee and love for the entire world.

We need to understand that in the gradual process, we leave ourselves as individuals and perceive more and more relations with expanding circles of humanity. This brings us more wisdom, feeling, and mingling with others. From that mingling we perceive the whole of reality until we feel the whole of Nature. In this way, by exiting ourselves and feeling everyone else, we comprehend the new reality in which we live.

This is the existence on the human, speaking level, which Nature has prepared for us. This is how we properly conduct our existence here in this world.

We must preserve the still, vegetative, and animate, and love Nature. We need to relate to natural things with balance. Loving Nature means that we live in it, not that we take from it as much as we can.

We need to understand what it means to live in balance, to feel it within ourselves, to feel balanced among us. Being in balance means preserving everything and taking from Nature only what is needed for existence, as do animals. Integral education is what compels us to treat the whole of the surrounding Nature well. Through our connection with it, we will learn how to relate to one another positively. This is why we needn't teach ourselves to be in good relations except as part of the Integral Education, which relates to the whole of Nature.

The term "Nature" means that we are evolving. Something is moving us, developing us. Where do the forces that develop us come from? We can see there is a gradual process here: Nature is developing us through a cause-and-effect process, where everything is interdependent. This is Nature's encompassing formula.

These things are known to science, as is the mutual impact among all parts of Nature. We didn't invent anything. We are only learning from ourselves how we can unite in order to be one with all of Nature and with the general law of Nature that develops us and the rest of Nature.

The law of Nature develops not just me or human society, but the entire universe. We don't know in which direction, but it's a fact that the universe is developing and expanding, and there are processes within it we have yet to understand.

The more we advance, the more we see that there is a vast system of laws in play. In the end, we see that all the laws we are discovering are linked, except that we can't see the connections between the laws of biology, zoology, botany, astronomy, or psychology. Although we can't see the connections, Nature is single and uniform. There are no divisions in it; this is a fact we learn from our studies.

Life, too, necessitates that we relate to matters in a holistic manner. The word "whole" comes from the Greek word, "holism," and we are parts of that single whole.

Because our evolution should be from the love of Man to the love of Nature, I can develop a good attitude toward human society, and with that attitude I can destroy the Earth. Conversely, I might preserve Nature and not people, like environmentalists who care only about ecology.

Our attitude toward things should be uniform, round. There must be one attitude toward everything. Because Man is part of Nature, we must have the same attitude toward the human society, toward a person, a family, and toward Nature as a whole. We must balance all parts of Nature because this is what exists in Nature. This is how we come to keep that general law.

Just as all the stars and planets are in balance moving in their tracks and affecting one another, and just as actions on one side of the planet affect the other side, this is how we should relate to others. Educating others to be in good human relations applies to the attitude toward the inanimate, vegetative, and animate as well, because we feed on them. That same attitude of balance should apply to the general law of Nature, which sustains and develops the whole of reality. This is the engine by which everything exists.

When we study Nature, we study the particular laws of a comprehensive law that scientists are still striving to reach. Scientists are trying to find the formula that will express the law of Nature in its entirety. This is what Einstein and others wanted so badly to feel, understand, examine, and see. Scientists feel that there is such a thing, without which there wouldn't be existence.

This is where humanity is being drawn. Man is drawn to attain his present place, and then understand where he is. We have a drive to know where we are, what we are really like, and what moves us, because our future depends on it. It determines our past and our fate. If my actions match my development, I will succeed. I will be able to promote myself and perhaps accelerate my development. However, if I go in the opposite direction, or turn to another direction that is not the direction of development, I will lose accordingly.

We can often say where a child will succeed and where he or she won't. To the extent that we understand the laws, we can explain to a child, according to its nature, conditions under which he or she exists and what possibilities are available. We also explain which options would succeed and which would not. In this way, we keep children from making critical mistakes.

The same applies to us. We want to move in the right direction and avoid making mistakes. This is the essence of development in science.

Indeed, development in science is not merely building new cellular phones. Rather, its goal is to understand the essence of our lives—why we exist, and how to improve our existence. We see that, for all our capabilities, we've come to a desperate state that shouldn't have happened. Therefore, knowing the general law and moving toward it will certainly bring us much closer to understanding where to move from here and how to build ourselves positively and practically, so it fits our lives and the lives of our children.

Scientists and many others speak of balance. This is not just my personal opinion. I am talking about the general, global Nature, in which there are scientific laws. The sciences show that in the end we see that everything is connected, "round."

It is a fact that we are in the midst of a global crisis, which we did not believe would happen. We thought we could do whatever we wanted, but all of a sudden we realized this wasn't the case. We can't do whatever we wish because we are all connected. Today, we live and feel the world as global; we feel Nature's global essence in everything, in the bank account, in our health, and in the world situation.

Today, all the scientists consider physics and chemistry connected. Nature has always been this way, but we've begun to understand it only in the last few decades. This is the influence of the environment on Man, and Man's influence on the environment. Today we see that everything is one. We see Man's influence on the climate, on the oceans, and on Nature as a whole, and we understand that Man should achieve balance with Nature.

We also need to balance our bodies, our health. We consume many things that ruin our bodies, and there are types of foods that we create only to make someone rich. The result is that hospitals fill with patients. Diabetes, for examples, is caused by excessive consumption of sugar. There is hardly any sugar in Nature. Rather, there is fruit and honey, but no raw sugar.

Humanity needs to examine everything it does and gradually rid itself of all toxic products. First, we will need to offer substitutes, but ultimately we will have to take them out completely. Just as we fight smoking, we will fight anything that's harmful to our bodies and our health. In Nature, there are fruits and vegetables, meat, fish, and water. Anything that doesn't exist directly in Nature is bad and harmful to the body. The point is that we need to understand that if something exists in Nature, we can find good use for it. If it doesn't exist in Nature, using it will certainly harm us.

This doesn't mean we need to become vegans or eat only organic foods without pesticides, hormones, or steroids. We have no choice but use them or we wouldn't be able to feed the whole of humanity and people would starve. We need to use those stimulants, but we also need to initiate studies and gradually replace what we're creating through genetics and chemistry with other things.

For example, there are places where chemicals are not used as pesticides. Instead, the natural enemies of the pests are brought in to eat the pests. There is much we can do, but first we need to make sure everyone has food, and then gradually progress in order to avoid hurting the ecology. This is why change needs to happen through Integral Education, which will lead us into balance and correction in all areas of life. In this way we will develop a good, balanced attitude toward everything we do, and revolutionize our attitudes in every realm of life, including agriculture and the economy.

We need to educate ourselves through the environment and establish for ourselves the right environment, which will show each of us his or her desirable, progressive form. People will come under the influence of the environment and change, as we get our desires from the environment.

Take architecture, for example. Assume that I'm indifferent to this profession. However, I am told that this profession can bring me some very special benefit, so I study architecture and go to architecture events, conferences, and conventions. In those events, everyone is talking about the importance of this profession, how to build this kind of a house, that kind of a house, and share their great ideas. I hear all that and become included in it.

All of a sudden, I stop being indifferent. The inclusion affects me and I begin to absorb their desires. Thus, I have changed. Previously, I had no desire for it, but now I suddenly find myself taking interest, having an opinion, and continuing my architecture studies.

This is how we get desires. From where do we acquire desires for things like science, knowledge, or a certain profession? We acquire them by seeing them in the world around us. A villager who lives in a remote, isolated village without Internet or TV will know that he could become something that has to do with agriculture. These are the professions he knows. Out of these choices he will choose what is best for him. Thus, everyone learns through the environment.

Also, the environment impresses and affects every person according to one's nature. I remember that my father wanted me to be a musician. He wouldn't let me watch kids' movies, and instead, took me to the movies to watch films about great composers like Mozart and Beethoven.

To be honest, I didn't find anything desirable about their lives: Mozart got sick and died when he was 35, and Beethoven became deaf. What I did receive, however, was an appreciation of these people; I appreciated what they did, and that they sacrificed themselves for their great desire to compose great music. That impression remained with me although it didn't make me want to be like them, since I was being impressed otherwise through my unique nature. Another person might have been impressed and wished to become a composer, too. Everyone is impressed by the environment and according to one's nature.

To summarize, there is only one thing we need to do: "Love covers all crimes." That is, we're all criminals, and over all our crimes we need to spread the canopy of love. This is how we will obtain balance with Nature, and then we'll have no problems and no bad feelings. We will feel ourselves above the still, vegetative, and animate, above our current lives, on a level that is all love and perfection, and this is also what we'll leave for our children.

CHAPTER TWELVE

Overuse of the Power of Reception Causes the Crisis

HOW TO ACQUIRE THE POWER OF BESTOWAL FROM THE ENVIRONMENT

Thus far, we've been evolving through the power of reception. That force has been pushing us forward and developed in us a desire to receive for ourselves, acquire, understand, know, dominate, and also to envy other people, meaning want what others have for ourselves.

We've acquired knowledge about the world, learned to integrate ourselves in it, and now we're quite proficient about everything in it, and dominate it. However, now we must balance our force of reception with the other force that exists in Nature, the force of bestowal. Being constantly under the dominance of the force of reception—the harmful and detrimental force—creates imbalance in Nature, in the environment, in man, and in human society.

For this reason, we must acquire the power of bestowal, the power of giving and participating. The force of bestowal can develop into the greatest power of love. Man can develop that power only through free choice, by designing an environment that will constantly give him an example by which he will change. Knowing the force of bestowal and its benefits will help us understand our lives and reality in general far beyond our current knowledge.

If we consider our development since birth, we will see that initially we develop by receiving knowledge about the world from our parents, or from people who are close by our cradle. As we grow we learn from examples given by our educators on how to manage in life. When we are grownups and ready for life, we keep gaining knowledge and skills for managing in the world through our environments, and through the events and situations we experience. That is, we act with the power, knowledge, and preparation from our infancy and childhood, and as grownups we have our own children whom we educate and prepare for life.

This is how we develop. Clearly, without knowing the world, we will not be able to survive in it. The more we know and can use our knowledge in life, the more we will develop and succeed. Our success depends on how much knowledge we will acquire about the world. This is why we try to pass on to our children the valuable information we've acquired, to provide them with the ability to persevere.

After developing for thousands of years, and especially in the last fifty or sixty years, we are beginning to see the end of our egoistic development. We see that it's impossible to advance having one desire—to receive, to acquire, to draw abundance to ourselves, while being inconsiderate of others and of Nature. Additional desires are appearing in us: we want to understand more, feel more, to "penetrate" our world. Our powers aren't enough. They are ruining us and the environment, and they're ruining the whole of Nature around us.

This is why our awareness of the other force we're missing, the power of giving, is now awakening. In truth, this is the force that's actually "running" the world. It is the great force of "Mother Nature" from which evolution stems, because everything happens by the power of giving, the force of bestowal. Like parents toward their children, Nature tends to us. However, we enjoy it because we receive everything from it, but we are not at all like it.

If we consider the essence of our lives, the process we are going through while evolving, and the purpose we should reach, we will see that every development in Nature has its purpose. If we wish to know the purpose, we need to know Nature better, to study and to understand the forces acting in it, and then we can understand what is happening to us, and contemplate how to evolve into a truly good and peaceful life.

If we begin to think in this way, we will see that all of Nature operates in two forces—a giving force and a receiving force. The giving force is the force of bestowal, consideration, bonding, and ultimately the general power of love.

The power of love includes all the positive forces in all the degrees of Nature—still, vegetative, animate, and speaking. These are the forces that give life, good influence, and pull us toward bonding and sustaining. We evolve specifically through those two forces.

If we examine our body, or anything else in the universe, we will see that it is governed by forces. By the connection of those two forces since the onset of the universe, they began to create a form that is neither one of them. This is how matter was formed. The forces of bestowal and reception began to evolve together, creating negative and positive particles, electrons and protons, which although opposite, together created the atom. The atoms connected into bigger blocs, forming crystals, which are forms of matter in the still nature.

Subsequently, the still nature received conflicting forces—positive and negative, giving and receiving—in such a way that they began to increasingly mingle with one another in order to bond. The negative forces wished to receive from the positive forces, and the positive forces gave to them. Thus, through a kind of mutual complementation, the living cell was formed. That cell became a receiving force in and of itself, by receiving or absorbing substances and energy from the environment.

In other words, again we see the two forces constantly acting in mutuality. This is how life evolved, by combining those forces which are in a constant dynamic between them. When the dynamic between them grew far more complex, these forces created living matter. In the animate, living matter, there are very clear data that are passed by heredity from generation to generation.

That combination of forces also happens in the vegetative and in the still, although in them it's harder for us to notice it. In animals, we see how a living organism forms out of the energy that exists in the embryonic cell. The cell absorbs materials from the outside, and by absorbing, emitting, and combining those materials according to pieces of information within which are conflicting data between the two forces, the living body is created.

In the inanimate, vegetative, and animate nature, everything develops through combinations of the two forces. We can see in Nature gradual, instinctive development according to a predetermined plan embedded within every being. They evolve according to the laws within them, and according to the environment. As the environment changes, their evolution changes. In the end, primarily on the human level, we see that the giving, supporting, providing force of Nature is more concealed, deeper, while the receiving force is the force of Nature that develops, and is more conspicuous and evident.

The more one receives, the more one grows. In the still, vegetative, and animate, reception follows an inner program, and it is similar in the human. Man, who's been evolving for hundreds of thousands of years, goes through the same evolution as do animals. However, if we examine the state we are in today, it seems that our evolution as animals has come to an end, and we are shifting toward a different mode.

We've exhausted all the receiving force within us. We've come to a state where we cannot develop through it any longer, and now we really need the giving force in Nature, which is appearing now on the part of the general bestowal, on the part of giving, and even on the part of love.

Following our study of Nature, we are discovering that Nature is round, global, integral, as though we exist in a sphere. Nature is increasingly presented to us as inclusive, giving. Accordingly, we feel that we are opposite from it, that we must use all the treasures given to us in a manner that is in balance with Nature. And yet, we can't, because the force of bestowal is absent in our behavior, in our development, in our knowledge.

How is it possible to acquire knowledge about this power? It is possible in the same way we received information from our parents, educators, and the environment about the proper use of the receiving force, meaning how we can receive more out of life and succeed. This is how we should learn to receive from the environment information about the other force, Nature's original force, the source of Nature, the giving force, the power of bonding, the power of love.

During our development, we've always used the power of separation. We've compared ourselves to others, desiring to be superior to them, more successful, and above them. As we previously worked successfully with the power of reception, now we must improve ourselves and acquire the other force, the power of bestowal and giving, and know how to work with it, and how to combine those two forces together.

We are currently in a special situation that enables us to receive information about the other force and learn what we can acquire through it. We can find examples for it even in our egoistic world, which is built around the force of reception.

The force of reception in the still, vegetative, and animate is an instinctive force by which one consumes the other. In Man, that force exists excessively, so Man wants to receive and use the entire world for his delight, not taking anyone else into consideration. But still, within our environment, within our society, there is an example of the two opposite forces: there is "me" and there is "the other," "me" and the "environment," "me" and "humanity."

Through relations between me and the others, through others' impact on me, I will be able to organize an environment, study the force of bestowal, the power of bonding, and the power of giving, versus the power of receiving. Thus, if we properly arrange psychology as a science that researches man's relations with the human environment, we will be able to start receiving clear data and information about the power of bestowal, and study it atop the power of reception we've acquired thus far. We will be able to learn that we oppose the environment. If it is a good environment that favors advancement, it will show me what is the force of bestowal. And although I will not want it, it will affect me through its values that it's in my best interest to adopt its values because otherwise I'll disappoint myself and degrade myself. I will be expelled from that environment, something that no one wants.

Through the same qualities of envy, lust, and honor, the environment begins to affect me and I begin to feel that I have no choice but to adapt myself to it. In this way, I'll gain its respect and appreciation, rather than disgrace and expulsion. This leaves an egoistic person only one choice, to position himself in a respectable manner in relation to the environment in order to feel great and respected.

We can certainly arrange our studies and the connection with the environment in such a way. If the environment is managed by the proper educators, it can teach each of us so we may begin to truly feel the force of bestowal and how special it is.

In this way, we will consider our environment as stages in our education. The environment will be to me as parents are toward a baby. I will be influenced by it as if by loving and caring parents who provide me with abundance and understand all my wants and weaknesses.

Thus, gradually, through small influences by a considerate, merciful environment, I will grow and seemingly become a youth, although I'm actually an adult. A person goes through these stages of development like a baby, then like a child, then like a youth.

According to the stages of development, the environment affects and nurtures us. It also demands that we be more giving toward it and work together with it in a combination of states to bring us, through mutual relations, into mutual bestowal.

Afterwards, when I have grown enough, I will understand that the forces of bestowal can work in my favor, that through them I can give to the environment. Then I, too, become an element in this environment, as any of the others who are in it. I become an equal member in that environment, and we all treat each other in a balanced manner so the force of reception and the force of bestowal are balanced between us. Thus, gradually, such an environment develops.

The environment indeed develops. So much so that the force of bestowal becomes the dominant force among us that determines all our actions, all of our relations, all our thoughts, and all of our intentions toward each other.

In this way, we build a safe, healthy society that doesn't waste, and form a kind of family where each of its members cares for the others. In that state, life will certainly seem different compared to the dysfunctional families we see today.

In addition, we will be acquiring the power of bestowal. To the extent that we acquire it, we will begin to relate to Nature as a mother to us. We will grow by the power of bestowal we will have gradually acquired, a kind of bestowing baby, bestowing child, bestowing youth, and bestowing grownup toward the environment. Now we are beginning to be like Nature, feeling the inner forces that exist within it, the forces behind matter.

If we decompose matter to its most basic elements, we will find atoms. If we split those, we will find particles. If we split the particles, we will find a force. In the end, this is what exists—a force. This is what physicists are finding in particle accelerators.

This is also how we acquire these fundamental forces— the force of bestowal and the force of reception—that exist at the basis of every matter. We permeate matter, creation, and begin to feel and understand how everything is built, how it is put together, and how everything is connected in amazing wisdom only by combining those two forces. Then we begin to understand more deeply what is behind those forces, how they operate, and the program that operates them.

As we study these forces with our intellect, we begin to acquire the inner wisdom that operates the whole of Nature. By doing so, we begin to connect and understand, truly *experience* the power, the inner program, the mechanism behind all of matter, behind all the particles, and behind everything that happens.

In other words, by acquiring these two forces of bestowal and reception so they are balanced in me, I come to know Nature, the Mother, the operating force that creates life, the force that leads life toward its purpose. It is then that I can also discover the purpose, and I gain a better understanding of my life and where I am. Everything becomes transparent; I penetrate all that is happening around and within me, and begin to see everything as combinations of the forces.

This is the knowledge I acquire. I don't acquire it superficially, as I previously acquired knowledge when I used only the force of reception. Rather, the combination of the two forces and the qualities I acquire grant me inner tools. These are not like the external tools that physicists, chemists, and other scientists use with their research instruments. Instead, I begin to feel the whole of Nature *within* me, and my self as an integral part of it.

In this way I begin to see, live, and integrate with this entire process. I begin to be *in* it. I also don't feel myself at the level of the solid, animate body, or at the levels of vegetative or still. Instead, I feel the forces that operate in the body, and how they equalize with the Nature that surrounds us, and are unified and connected to the general, global nature.

This is what I mean by "integral nature," that a person is really connected when finding the internal system of one's inner forces, the forces of the environment, and the whole of Nature. In that state, one really sees oneself as an integral part of this system and comes to know the laws of Nature, feeling the eternity and perfection that exist in Nature.

This is how we slowly detach from sensing ourselves. We become detached from the sensation we previously had in the solid, self-centered body when we were in conflict with the environment and the external conditions. By knowing and attaining, by this newly acquired awareness, we move into being in the realm of the inclusive, eternal, and perfect Nature, and rise to the degree of "human," which is similar to this vast system.

This is really the purpose of our evolution in the new era to which we have moved. The difference between this and the old era is in our new perception of life. In the previous era we progressed instinctively because we were operated by only a single force—that of reception—and worked only to receive as much as possible. Now we have to operate with the force of bestowal, and develop an attitude of consideration and increasing unity, to complement and integrate with others and with the environment.

These two forces in me complement each other at the human level. The force I am developing is the force of bestowal, of unity, consideration, and love. The other force is the force of reception within me, which grows and develops along with this process, though not in the way it has evolved thus far. Instead, it continues to develop opposite the force of bestowal.

I also gain better understanding of the creativity in the process because now I'm not developing as blindly as I did before, when I simply ran where the ego pushed me. Now I develop through understanding, sensing, attaining, through scrutiny, criticism, and corrections that I make. I achieve balance by combining, complementing, and connecting those two forces, similar to the balance that exists in atoms, molecules, and any living organism. Afterwards, "above" this balance, I uncover another deficiency, a need to find an even higher balance. Thus we continually develop from whole to even more whole.

The purpose of this process is to develop an awareness of who we are, and a knowledge of the system in which we exist. When we permeate Nature by balancing our inner forces, we begin to feel the stages that are hidden from us, the forces and spaces we currently cannot reach. We move into a system of forces that is above time, space, and motion, and reach such attainment and such internal fulfillment in our minds and hearts that have no connection to the existence of our bodies. Everything happens within the attainment, the awareness we acquire. Our bodies are only a manifestation of our initial, animate forces, allowing us to achieve the human degree.

This is why we need to recognize the importance of our time and the state we are in. We have come to a state of "delivering" ourselves as humans who are similar to Nature. Therefore, we have a beautiful and good development ahead of us, one of understanding and attainment, leading toward a good life without any limitations.

We need to be aware that we are not animals living inside a body and wanting only to satisfy it. We are not self-centered beings that need to satisfy the ego, which manipulates us into false goals that only pain us. An ancient maxim says, "One does not die with even half one's craving in one's hand." That is, no one is satisfied with life. When we pass away, we take nothing with us. Besides, today many of us truly have nothing, even while still alive.

However, in potential, we are sublime beings, the apex of Nature, which created and designed through this wondrous process the universe, Earth, evolution, and we humans.

Evolution must end in each person attaining the whole of Nature, becoming identical to it, in balance with it, in wholeness, unity, using all of our qualities in a mode of giving. That is, we must eventually use the force of giving just as Nature does. When we achieve that state, we'll see that our entire evolution has actually been a preparation for this. Even before Earth was created, all the forms of development of the ego in the world of reception—from inanimate, through vegetative, animate, and to the birth of humanity till this day—have been preparations for the evolution of the human species, now on the threshold of entering the new world of bestowal.

We see the balance between the two forces in our own bodies, and in all the systems we study in Nature. It is the balance on which the balancing of climate and various social systems such as economy and health depends. Balance means health. However, there are different levels of balance. On the inanimate level, balance brings tranquility. On the vegetative level, balance brings health, as it does on the animate level.

However, the balance is always dynamic, moving from smaller balance to greater balance. We need to look at the stages. For example, if we consider an apple growing on a tree, it grows from smaller balance to greater one until it ripens. However, even during its pre-ripening stages, it is in relative balance at each stage, until imbalance appears in it in relation to its next stage of ripening. This is how it develops and grows.

What do we need today, when humanity is like a rotten apple? What can we do to balance ourselves? What is the force we need in order to balance ourselves? We need the force of bestowal, which we should add to the force of reception, the force of the ego. If we balance those two forces, we will live in peace and good health for our families, countries, and in the entire world. This is all we need.

The only way to acquire the force of bestowal is through the right environment. We can teach any person how to acquire this force to help in one's personal and social life, and then to the whole of civilization.

For thousands of generations, we have been living in a world motivated by the force of reception. Now, our next step in human development is to shift to the world of giving, where the force of giving dominates, and by which our development is moved.

The force of giving exists also in the world of reception, but we've been using it to receive because there can be only one dominating force, and the question is, "Which force is that?" If the force of reception dominates, the force of bestowal serves it through our willingness to give a little in order to receive more.

Everything develops only to add to itself. In all of the still, vegetative, and animate in our world, as well as in Man, who is part of the animate, evolution has been via the dominance of the force of reception over the force of bestowal.

This is especially noticeable in Man because he is an egoist who has used the force of reception to harm others. In Man, it is evident how the force of reception dominates the force of bestowal. It also exists in lower degrees, in the still, vegetative, and animate, but is clearer in Man because it is more evident that we do everything *only* to satisfy ourselves, to gain.

By my own nature, I cannot do anything without the prospect of profit that comes with it, a profit that I will feel as pleasure, satisfaction, or a surplus to my investment. My investment is in giving, and what I receive must exceed the giving. This is the meaning of "the force of reception dominating the force of bestowal."

This is why we've come to such excessive use of the force of reception, which dominates the force of giving, where we want only to profit from everyone unreservedly. That is, I'm willing to sell to anyone and everyone, destroy everything for an ounce of satisfaction, an ounce of pleasure, with no consideration for anyone in any way, shape, or form. It's not that it is good or bad, but the result of the process is this unreserved reception at the height of our egoistic development, and it is true for every single person.

Once we have reached such a level that the difference between the forces of reception and bestowal became so great, we detached them from one another. This is why we feel we're in a crisis and cannot continue to exist. Now, the force of bestowal is so far from the force of reception it can no longer help us develop. The ego has grown so large that we want everything for ourselves. The ego doesn't allow us to perform any act of giving, not even for personal gain. The ego doesn't let me tolerate anyone next to me, so I avoid starting a family and raising kids because I'd have to pay for it with concessions, consideration, and mutual giving, and I'm not willing to do that.

We see that the force of reception has outgrown the force of bestowal in every realm of life. At every point, my thought is only how to maximize my benefits. This is how we distort the rules and create all kinds of rules that allow us to steal legally.

The relations we have built among us are such that we have no consideration for anyone, not for our families, for our kids, for society, for the country, or for humanity. This is why there is a crisis in humanity, in culture, and in Nature. How does the crisis manifest in Nature? We're throwing trash into the ocean or into dumpsters and expect others to clean up after us.

Our egos don't let us think about tomorrow because they always check only what we have here and now. Without immediate gain, we don't care what will happen. Thus, unlike before, when economists planned for five, ten, and even twenty years ahead, today we cannot even predict what will happen tomorrow. Our indifference has brought us into disorientation. The ego has broken down our systems, and even the connection we once had between the force of bestowal and the force of reception doesn't exist anymore. Because of this, we won't be able to survive.

But when we look at the process of evolution, we can anticipate its end because, as the saying goes, "The wise, his eyes are in his head." We don't need to get to a point where we destroy one another to realize it's not in our interest to continue this way. It is similar to a clever child who learns from warnings how to behave, instead of suffering punishments. As we said, "Who is wise? He who sees the future."

The solution is to create within our social system a structure that will help us, push us, and will always teach us how to increase our force of bestowal, without which there is no life. The force of bestowal is the power of unity, connection. Today our connections to our families and the human society are weakening. In the end, we're putting ourselves and society to death because we're not using this force.

Today acquiring that force is a must, a matter of life and death. This is why the crisis is happening, to show us where we are. It is showing us that we have built that state, and now we need to scrutinize it, check it, and see that we need the force of bestowal.

We acquire such a force through building a good environment, one that gives us an example, pressures us, and encourages us to be a little more giving. Such a society relates to each of us, seemingly pointing and saying, "If you don't bestow, you won't receive. And not only will you not receive, you will lose the feeling that you have today."

Society should express discontent with anyone who is not giving, and must affect a person through the ones near him and the ones important to him. It needs to act toward each and every person through the sensation of respect, one's sense of self-esteem, and one's "human" sensations. Society will show disrespect if one is not giving, even to the point of expelling that person.

In this way we will force people to contemplate acquiring the force of bestowal. When we learn what the force of bestowal is, when we want to acquire it, society will give us lots of favorable attitude and appreciation. We have no choice; we need to learn what it means to bestow.

When I come to my studies, I want society to affect me on two levels: on the one hand, with a stick against my ego, expressing scorn toward the quality of my reception, and on the other hand with a carrot, encouraging me and appreciating the force of bestowal that I will acquire. Then I begin to appreciate, in my ego, the force of bestowal, which is opposite to it, since if I implement this force, I will receive fulfillment from the appreciation of the environment.

In other words, we manipulate the ego, which is growing and is excessive in each of us. We can implement such education only through the environment. This is called "Integral Education." When we educate people into being integral, connected, and tied to everyone else, they begin to appreciate the force of bestowal. Then, through the force of bestowal, they acquire for themselves an environment that respects them.

When a person is appreciated and respected, people envy that person, seeing how much he or she has risen and become valued by society. When that happens, one begins to appreciate the force of bestowal because by showing people that he or she has this force, one receives high social status and respect.

What happens is that through the right environment, an egoist begins to appreciate the force of bestowal. To the extent that one acquires this force, a person begins to show it to the environment. This is yet another demonstration of the power of the environment.

The environment is like an educator, like an adult's behavior toward a youth, like parents toward their baby, like a teacher toward a student, or like the human society toward each of us. Society relates to a person according to that person's progress. By using the forces of reception and bestowal toward the environment, a person acquires a means by which to permeate oneself, society, and Nature. Through it, one begins to understand what is happening to him or her at the level of forces. This is the inner psychology of us, the environment, and Nature.

As we explore ourselves, we begin to feel how those two forces actually operate in the whole of reality, how they affect the still, vegetative, and animate within us, in the environment, within a family, in everything. We begin to work with the two forces as though we are their owners, and through them we study and see everything. We enter the network connecting the whole of reality because that network is a web of those two forces.

Then a person understands the purpose of the whole of Creation, the entire process that he or she went through, and where it is leading. We can see that everything is going through a certain process, though we cannot currently discern it because we only have one force, that of reception. When we begin to use both forces, we acquire a tool by which to examine, much like scientists, all that is happening in Nature. We become masters of our own destinies, and of everything that's happening. And it all happens simply by raising our awareness.

Our inability to use the balance between the two forces—that of reception and that of bestowal—leads us into disorientation. This is a direct result of our inconsideration of others. "Inconsideration" means that I am not balanced between the force of bestowal and the force of reception within me, and hence cannot be considerate toward others.

Therefore, because of my imbalance between these forces, I don't perceive where I am because I'm looking through my instrument. If that instrument is warped and not calibrated, I see the world with twisted eyes and don't understand what is happening.

We can see this among rulers, economists, and financiers who can't seem to find their way in our world. They are doing all they can to postpone the inevitable gloomy end, but are only leading us to a much worse situation. Millions of people will take to the streets and riot, which might lead to wars, even world wars, pandemics, and natural disasters.

If we're speaking of the world of forces, then we are the ones with the greatest power. When we acquire the superior balancing power at the human level, we understand that we are at the top of the system.

When we are balanced within, we balance out all the levels of the still, vegetative, and animate in the whole of reality because Man is at the highest level of power and awareness, and the balancing power in the subtlest force in Nature—the power of thought. All the other forces are at a lower level than the power of thought. They are material forces activated by the power of thought, which does not relate to the power of our thought, but a power of thought that is present in Nature. It relates to the overall plan, the engine that works and turns everything into one.

We are now at a very special point in our development. Thus far, Nature has been controlling us and has brought us to the lowest point in our development. From here on we have to start ascending and acquire the force that exists in Nature—the power of balancing between good and bad.

We need to acquire the will to bestow in order to have two forces in our hands, bestowal and reception. If we receive that instrument, the ability to combine the two forces, we will begin to dominate the whole of Nature, since we are in that system. Thus, we become a living, active part in it, moving and evolving, giving life to the entire system.

According to the force of bestowal that a person develops, the force of reception grows in him again. It is no longer that small egoistic force of the animate level, which one used in the old world. Now the two forces are developing in him together, the forces of Man in the new world. Thus far, Man has developed instinctively, like an animal, reaching an intolerable level. Now he is about to develop the force of bestowal toward the environment.

Giving, or bestowing, includes giving, consideration, closeness, support, kindness, and finally, love. Love includes all expressions of connection. Sympathizing with another's wish is called "the force of bestowal." As soon as I begin to develop that force in me, next to it grows the other force, that of reception, which actually helps me bestow because within me, there is nothing to give to others. I have nothing with which to connect to them. Rather, it is precisely when I use all my forces of reception that I can give the most to others. I was created by Nature as a force of reception that's been evolving since the beginning of the universe to this day. The question is, "How do I begin to bestow upon others?" It is possible only if I'm in a society that says, "If you're not bestowing, we won't accept you, we won't appreciate you, we will simply not want you because you don't have good values." It is a society that makes me feel that all my relatives, the people around me, and all those I care about won't appreciate me unless I bestow. And once I get this treatment and attitude from everyone, I begin to understand that it's in my interest to bestow.

To summarize, by acquiring the force of bestowal I become aware of what is happening around me, I tend to myself and my family, and to the near and far society, and I arrange my life ideally.

Thus, I reach a state of happiness and sensation of the eternal reality. I am included in it, and I achieve the human degree. I feel that life is worth living, that I want to have a family, and I experience satisfaction and contentment. It all happens by acquiring the force of bestowal built in me by being in the right environment.

CHAPTER THIRTEEN

From Hate to Love

HOW TO BUILD OURSELVES AS HUMANS

Nature is setting before us a necessary condition for our existence: We must achieve a state of perfect love. But can we meet this condition and achieve all-inclusive love among all seven billion people living in the world today? If we obtain only part of it or move toward achieving that goal, will we see how that condition acts in our favor and changes our lives and the entire environment in our favor?

Our current nature is for everyone to care only for oneself. We cannot think of anything or anyone else. If we study Nature, we will discover that even the slightest movement, such as moving my hand from one place to another, requires energy. That energy is at my disposal on condition that I receive some benefit from the movement.

In other words, the condition for any movement, from the atomic and molecular levels through the movements of the body, and onto the mind and heart, requires that the outcome will be better than the previous state. This is how I relate to every action in my life.

There are things I do instinctively. For example, I don't think about how I should sit or talk; it's an inner calculation. But the majority of my actions are affected by the presence of an egoistic desire that, at the end of each act, I will experience a good feeling.

The desire to feel good creates and designs my every movement, determines how I conduct myself, where I go, what I do, how I speak, and how I behave. Each act happens only in order to improve my situation. When I want to sleep, eat, walk, talk, work, it is only to obtain self-gratification. In other words, I cannot think of anything but my own benefit.

In fact, my whole life is an attempt to obtain maximum benefit, to suffer less and enjoy more. I want to receive and fill myself with all that I can.

This state is a result of education, influence of an environment, good or bad values that I received naturally, or habits that have become second nature. I was accustomed to having to keep things even when they're unnatural, and I exist through them. Many actions in my life stem from a habit to which I grew accustomed through society, parents, and educators. That is, I perform those actions not because I initially wanted to do them; I do them automatically.

In much of my conduct, I'm not even required to do any thinking. The body, an autonomous system, performs the majority of my actions.

There are actions I perform out of inner effort, where I convince myself that it's worth my while. For example, when the alarm goes off and I want to keep sleeping, I still force myself to get up and go to work. It may be hard, uninteresting work, but I know that after all the work is done, I will return to a warm house and a loving family where I can rest and feel good. So in the end, working is worthwhile for me.

All my connections with certain people, or disconnections from other people, are made in order to feel better. I'm constantly occupied with trying to feel better. It's my nature; it's the nature of each and every one of us. That nature is a basic nature at the animate level. The still, vegetative, and animate are constantly drawn to feel better, to be in a better state that will seem to them as balanced, where they feel no pressure or pull toward either side, but rather feel in harmony with what seems like a better life.

It follows that throughout my life, I'm constantly honoring the law, "How to feel better." We exist under this condition, and my egoistic nature constantly directs me toward that state.

This brings up the question, "If I'm so concerned with myself throughout my life, internally, instinctively, and consciously, how will I be able to change my nature into the opposite, into loving others?" True love of others is when my whole being is given to the other. I place myself at the service of others with all my physical abilities, my skills, and all the means at my disposal. I think of the other and care for others to the point that I have nothing left for myself. I follow the desire to bestow, to give to others, constantly making sure things are the best possible for them.

We can compare it to a mother caring for her baby. Nature directs and pushes her to constantly care for the baby so it feels good and safe. She has nothing in her life but concern for her child. She looks at it, wonders what she should feed it, how to clean it, when to put it to bed, what to do with it so it has everything of the best. She has no other concerns. But is it realistic to think that I need to relate to humanity with such devotion?

Also, if Nature has put this condition before us, why have we come to the complete opposite state, where we care only for ourselves? Moreover, even animals care only for themselves, and Man, more than the animals, wishes only to gain at the expense of others, exploit them, and impose himself and his view on them. Man enjoys being superior to others, wants to subjugate them and keep them under him. Man even enjoys others suffering a little more than he, and likes being in a better situation than the other.

We constantly test ourselves in relation to others. With this test in relation to the environment, we learn what our situation is compared to others. Yet, this brings up the question, "If my ego has brought me to a situation where I need others only so I can feel superior to them, how will I be able to invert my nature to the opposite?"

If I imagine a utopian situation in which I truly am concerned only with the well-being of others, like a mother toward her child, if I have such love and care for them, I may indeed feel complete self-realization. Yet, today I don't see how I can reach that state, so why should I commit to it?

Throughout history, love of others has been the basis of ethics, religions, and various social doctrines. Numerous books have been written about it. People tried to build favorable social circles centuries ago. There were attempts by Utopians to build villages, towns, and even countries on the basis of good relations among people. But the attempts failed.

During our evolution, we have become smarter, learned about human nature, and realized we couldn't rise above it. Even if we get something good and special in a utopian society that places love of others as its standard, it is impossible to build a society that actually implements it.

In fact, we have limited ourselves through rules of behavior so we wouldn't hurt each other. There are lawyers, sociologists, psychologists, and politicians who assist in creating the rules of the social environment.

We connect among us only to get better services, such as when cities tend to their residents' clearing of trash or building kindergartens, or educational and cultural institutes only to give us what we need. For that, we are willing to be considerate of everyone's needs when it pays us to unite, paying a little and receiving a service that costs far less when everyone shares its cost. Clearly, there is benefit in collective organizations. However, when changing one's *emotional attitude* is concerned, turning it into one of consideration of others, it is very difficult for us.

Today we are beginning to understand the crisis we are in. The crisis actually a crisis in our relations. All the egoistic forms we have been living in have brought us into building a society that is more convenient for everyone, out of consideration for everyone. And yet, we eventually realized that the number of dissatisfied people would be greater than those satisfied, leading to a collision between them that could lead to civil war. We understood that we needed to restrain our egos, so we wouldn't consume one another.

The relations among us have always been under the umbrella of egoism. We understood that this is our nature and that we must somehow restrain ourselves. Although there are many shades of our forms of egoism, to avoid eruptions that would ruin everything we have achieved, we needed a unifying mechanism. This is why humanity established such international organizations as the World Bank, the UN, etc., leading humanity into better discourse and consideration.

Especially over the last century, we've realized that we have no other choice but to be more considerate. After the two world wars we experienced, everyone realized that no one gains from these wars and that eventually everyone loses and pays a heavy toll.

This is why humanity has established different circles of connection, like the red button that allows Moscow and Washington to communicate in case of a threat of activating an atom bomb. The powers trust each other on that topic because they understand that no one will benefit from such an eruption. In fact, it is precisely due to the arms race and the understanding that there is no choice that they have established a form of communication and connection. On the one hand, it is an egoistic connection, but on the other hand, that development has brought us closer. Although we're even more hateful and want to kill one another, we are beginning to realize that the other side has the same power as we do, and we must take it into consideration.

The egoistic development deepened over the years through the connections made in industry and international trade. Businesses in developed countries realized that if they shifted their factories to less developed countries such as China or India, they would be able to find much cheaper labor than in their home countries. Thus, gradually, plants and factories moved from the West to Third World countries, where residents were trained to become workers. On the one hand, business owners increased their profits, but on the other hand, their countries were depleted of jobs and unemployment rose. The owners didn't care that those who worked for them became unemployed; their intention was to make a profit. As far as they were concerned, the government should take care of the unemployed.

When the government must see to the livelihood of millions of unemployed, the country becomes poor, goes into debt, and prints worthless money. The result of this process is that those developed countries in Europe and North America have become poor, with poor populations. This result is still not so evident, but it's an cumulative process that is gradually being exposed.

Worse yet, the owners of industry and international traders have grown richer and have strengthened their power by moving factories into poor countries. They made a twofold profit—making far more than what they were making in their home countries. These profits intensified their power, and once powerful, they began to affect politics in Europe and America.

So it happened that the ego rose to the top of the human pyramid, money became the most important, and the wealthy began to rule over everything. In the end, we've reached a financial, economic crisis, the last crisis that we are now beginning to experience.

But in this crisis, we are arriving not only at an economic crisis. We are also plunging into additional difficult situations to which the ego is leading us, precisely because those countries that were once developed have many destitute citizens. Society is disintegrating, education is being neglected, and the entire social system is falling apart.

The crisis is inclusive, global. All the countries are interconnected—the seemingly rich and the poor— that today manufacture most of the world's production. Everything that the third world produces must find buyers in the old, developed world. However, there are no buyers anymore because back there, people are now penniless. Thus, we can see that the crisis is only deepening.

Now we are arriving at a global world and a crisis that indicates the mutual connections among us. One of its symptoms is the ecological problem, caused by our race to produce and sell as much as we can, as long as we profit and make a few more billions that will lie idly in the bank. We thought this could go on forever, but the end has come because now that there are no more buyers, there is nowhere to expand. The result is a crisis that has affected education, culture, human relations, and is still expanding. Indeed, the heart of this crisis is human relations.

The crisis manifests in people struggling to survive. The sector that wants to manufacture can still progress, but there is no one to buy the products. The people in the developed countries that is now depleted and become penniless can no longer consume everything. In the past, it was a closed circle, a process of production and consumption: people produced and consumed what they themselves produced. Now, that circle doesn't exist.

The wealthy found a bogus solution: they began to play with money, even when there was no product, creating false demand for shares in the stock market. Thus, a financial bubble formed, made of economic bubbles that were pointless and had no reason to exist. In the end, we've reached yet another kind of crisis. Advertising and the game between the banks and the financial systems created a bogus economic reality.

Now the crisis is evident in all realms of life. We've come to a state where people can barely survive, and are in dire need. Young people fresh out of college want to start a family and make a respectable living. They want to make something of their lives, but soon they see that there is no demand for them and find themselves unemployed.

This phenomenon will worsen and continue to spread because as long as we are concerned only with ourselves and not with the world, we won't be able to provide even the staples to everyone. On one end of the world, huge amounts of food are thrown out, and on the other end, people are starving to death. Surplus food doesn't even reach nearby places that need it because the human ego doesn't care for others. Others don't matter unless they threaten us, and then, because we have no choice, we give them just enough to calm them down.

We can see it happening in the way the developed world is treating Africa. In the past, countries in Africa supported themselves, manufactured many things, and were a good source of raw materials. When products from Europe began to arrive there, they were deliberately far cheaper than local products. This ruined the local market, and people stopped making what they needed for their livelihood. Once the locals stopped working in their traditional professions, the countries that imported cheap products to Africa began to raise their prices because there was no competition from local manufacturers. This is how Africans became poor and destitute to this day. This is just one example out of many countries in a similar situation.

Now that we're in a global crisis caused by the human ego, we are beginning to feel the connection among everyone. The global crisis is felt in both developed countries and Third World countries, such as in Asia, where some of the countries have already started to develop, or Africa, where they are now destitute.

We are beginning to feel that we are all in the same boat. If one of us causes harm, we will all feel it and it will be impossible to advance. In fact, we're in a situation where our egos are returning to us like a boomerang with a negative feedback.

We can see it especially vividly in Europe, where countries connected by profiteering are stronger and more successful. An unbreakable connection has formed between them, and if one of the countries in the system, such as Greece, retires from the Common Market, it might cause all 26 other countries to fall. This perilous situation could bring the Common Market, the European society, the European Central Bank, and the Euro as its currency to a desperate situation, where no one can act without the agreement of all the others.

From the current situation, we realize that we must begin to be more considerate of one another. Indeed, there is animosity and a history of hostilities among us, forged by centuries of war and forceful domination of one nation over another. Yet, for lack of another choice, we're coming to a state where it is no longer enough to be considerate. We cannot continue to play by the rules of the egoistic society of the Common Market, rules we established out of our egoistic nature. It just doesn't work anymore.

Instead, we must act out of the inclusive, global nature, as does ecology, and out of the nature of Man. That is, both from within and from surrounding Nature, we feel we are faced with new conditions bearing on our existence that compel us to achieve love of others, and not merely egoistic consideration.

These words may sound unreal, far-fetched, even unacceptable, but we can approach love of others by building within ourselves a committing force. Instead of Nature forcing us to love others and be in mutual love, and in order to avoid starvation, disease, and natural disasters, we must build another force that will compel us to approach mutual love.

That force can exist only through an environment that we will organize to be more obliging than our own nature, and stand above economy, education, and food. That society will be so strong, and will resist our selfish hearts and our current nature. It will force us to change our attitudes toward others from hate to love. For that, we must toil to understand the kind of society we need.

It should be a society that encourages us through positive reinforcement and rebukes us if we don't come closer to each other. We will need to extol consideration, closeness, sympathy, mutual guarantee, and love so that these values can continue to develop among us.

Society needs to constantly explain how we should study human nature; then, we will develop society accordingly. We need to learn about the influence of the environment on each of us. Thus, we will be ready to change, know why we need to change, and find the strength to do it.

When I do something as easy as moving my hand from place to place, I still need energy to do it. Similarly, in our relations, I need to feel that positive encouragement is coming to me from Nature. I need to find it difficult to feel hatred, competition, remoteness, and repulsion that I may cause others, and I need to feel strong resistance to behave this way. Speaking kindly to others, consideration, mutual guarantee, and love will be quickly greeted with warmth, just like satisfaction and fulfillment. We need to build the environment so it provides me with these two forces—the bad force in response to my ego, and the good force in response to my love of others.

In building such an environment, we must take into consideration a quantitative force and a qualitative force that will convince, compel, caress, and warn each of us, and all of us together. Through joint participation in building this environment, we will build the new Nature that will affect us. We will complement the egoistic force that governs all of human nature with the good, altruistic force that is still not in us, and which we must nurture and develop.

Because we already understand the necessity for it, everything depends on how we organize, how much we commit ourselves and work on ourselves to convince one another to do so, using the media and every other system at our disposal.

We are already mingled in one another, but for now it is for egoistic motives. Here is where the magic words, "mutual guarantee," express the committed connection among us, which we must take into consideration. In such a connection of mutual guarantee, one who "drills a hole in the boat," or acts with egoistic motives, drowns everyone with him in the sea of egoism that is common to all.

Therefore, although it is an environment in which we are still egoistically connected, the mutual guarantee between us begins with our understanding how much the environment must teach us the necessity to shift our connections into altruistic ones. In mutual guarantee, we should feel like a family, where each person is everybody else's guarantor. Everything that anyone has or does affects everybody else. By studying our bad relations alongside our positive connections, we should gradually achieve new awareness, which will compel us to build good connections among us.

In this way we will understand that Nature has been promoting us for millennia toward this development, toward a situation known as a "crisis." The essence of the state of crisis is humanity's new birth, so we may come to that internal force that exists in Nature—the power of love—and balance with Nature by being in precise equilibrium with that force existing in the world.

The force of love that exists in Nature creates the still, vegetative, the animate, and Man. It is the force that gives life. If we acquire that power of love in relations, as in "Love your friend as yourself," we will actually acquire the general law of Nature, and we will realize it within us.

To implement that law, we must be opposite from it in order to feel how bad it is to be opposite from it. Through the contrast, as we rise out of the great ego into the great love, we will feel the gap between them. Through that gap, we will feel the wholeness, eternity, and greatness of the process we have been through. We will attain it in our perception and we'll understand how high, strong, eternal, and complete it is.

As there is no good without bad, and no sweet without sour, everything that delights us, everything we obtain in life, and all that we appreciate is always measured by comparing it to its opposite. This is why we measure everything by comparing it to other things. It's not enough to have a good feeling; I need to have a little more than the person next door. I could live on pennies a day as long as I had a penny more than my neighbor. This is what gives us fulfillment, that we are successful. Currently, this is the most important thing for us.

That law acts in the same way. If we achieve love, we measure it compared to the hatred that preceded it. Through the ratio between them, we feel how much we've gained, how much we've grown, how much our fulfillment has increased today compared to the situations we've been through over time, which are all in humanity's collective memory. This is when we achieve the perfect pleasure and fulfillment.

Implementing the condition of love of others will bring us to the perfect state, pleasure, and complete fulfillment. The energy to perform these actions toward shifting ourselves from egoism into love comes from two sources. On the one hand, Nature is compelling us to achieve balance and harmony among us. To do that, it is using blows that threaten our existence.

On the other hand, there is that positive force of the environment, which we build artificially, and which pulls all of us to become mutually integrated with it in a connection of mutual guarantee and love.

We're going through these processes in order to eventually come to know the Law of Love that exists in Nature, until we implement that law within us. All the previous forms exist so we can identify in them the opposite form, the purposelessness, the great shattering we are in. Through this shattering we will build the beautiful mechanism called "Man" by ourselves.

To summarize, the question is how to build ourselves as humans. We ourselves must build the environment that changes our situation from hate to love. We must measure and study ourselves, study the laws of Nature and the human society, learn how we should conduct ourselves, and decide what relations should prevail among us. Accordingly, we will build the society, the environment, and adapt ourselves to it. In effect, we are "taming" ourselves. That is, by taming our egos, we become its owners and hence become "human."

The human in us is not the still, vegetative, or animate levels. These are our foundations. It is also not another kind of egoistic development. Being "human" means that we need to make ourselves *humane* and do it by ourselves. We need to "give birth" to that human and raise that level within us. No one can do it for us. We received egoistic forces, but we're the ones who design the system that educates us.

We elevate ourselves through the degrees of love. As we ourselves change the environment, it, in turn, changes us. In this way, we work together, at each stage checking on the development of the improved, corrected self, and thus advance. According to the stages, we build an environment that will affect us into moving to the next level.

No one can do it alone. I can't pull myself out of the swamp by my own hair. The condition for success is therefore the construction of an outside force that will affect me, that will not let me escape, and will force me to bestow either pleasantly or unpleasantly. This is the only way that I can do it.

Nature is presenting us with a new, inclusive condition for survival. It is appearing in our consciousness as a crisis that makes it seem we're about to be destroyed, and there is no way out. Nature is presenting us with our general situation, and within it we must build by ourselves all the good situations by using the influence of the environment on each of us, even while we are the ones building this environment.

In the process, I check who I am, what I am, what is the nature I am in, what is my character, and what are my predilections. According to all the above, I build an environment that will compel me to meet the new conditions for existence that Nature is presenting to me, compelling me to agree to such a change out of my awareness of the goal.

Therefore, first we need to establish education. People need to understand that there is no other choice, just as we tell children that they must get an education in order to succeed in life. We are being born into a New World. To be born into it, each of us and all of us together must be persuaded to relate to one another and to the environment differently.

We need to recognize that what we are and what is around us are all parts of us, and we need to obtain that realization by ourselves. This is called "building a human being."

For example, in the past, dogs were like wolves. Over time, Man tamed the dogs until they became loyal to Man. Dogs then turned from enemies into friends. Similarly, I need to treat my ego like a dog that I must tame and change.

Therefore, I "split" myself into two—the new awareness, which is the human in me, and my ego, which is the dog. The relation between the two allows me to build my new self.

We can tame ourselves by ourselves and maximize our potential to evolve as humans by building the right environment that will compel us to "wrap" our egos with the opposite envelope, one that is good for our existence.

Each person should be aware of the key points in Integral Education, that there is a special process in creating a special reality. We truly are building a human being, and we're doing it by keeping the law, "Love your friend as yourself," which is Nature's inclusive law that we must reach today.

Particularly now, we have an opportunity to discover the overall Law of Nature because our egos have exhausted their development. We've come to a state where we are ready for correction. All we need is to affect our egos so they take on a human form, using an additional, external force that we build by ourselves through society. By so doing, we will implement the overall force of Nature and discover its full depth, vitality, eternity, magnitude, and the inclusive harmony within it.

Thus, we will slowly part from the life of "dogs" and achieve the level of humans, where we will remain. We will attach ourselves so strongly to the human level that our bodies, our lives, and all that we've been through over history will be but a prelude, a preparation for what we will attain henceforth. This is why we regard the current crisis as labor pangs of a new, enlightened world.

CHAPTER FOURTEEN

The Woman in the Connected World

WOMEN AS THE LEADING FORCE IN THE NEW WORLD

When examining the corrected society in which we want to live, much attention should be given to the family unit. The family will be a microcosm of the world we live in. Clearly, the right progress will create good family relations and good relations with the next generation.

In the society of the new world, we're meant to build the economy and the job market in sync with maintaining our families, the home, and the children's education. There is no doubt that women will play a key role in promoting the personal development of each member of the family, and the development of society.

Women are a force to be reckoned with. They constitute more than 50% of the world's population, and the power and abilities of women are unquestioned. Women can manage the household, family, relations with the husband, relationships among the children, and her own relationships with each of the kids. The woman is a mother, a wife, a teacher, an educator, the household economist, and the economist of her husband and kids. As a mother, the woman is also the spiritual essence of the family, complementing with education the information that children acquire at school.

The woman is the one person pouring meaning and spirit into her children through the internal wisdom that she passes on to her family. The woman is a source of education, culture, and knowledge, which she passes on to her children.

We must ascribe great significance to the pillar of the family, the woman. We should put women on a pedestal in all media outlets by extolling her place in the family, in particular, and in society, in general. The new reality will require us to establish new frameworks that support a fundamental role that has been eroded over the last century—the woman's role.

The more society praises, extols, and ascribes importance to the woman's role in the connected world, and the more we treat it as a career in and of itself—requiring particular training—the more women will succeed in their roles as women, wives, and mothers. Our gain will be people who are better qualified for societal life, and a better society as a whole.

Due to the decline of the woman's role in the family, the family unit—the human cornerstone—has greatly declined.

It stands bare and unprotected without its supporting pillar, and with it shakes the whole of civilization founded on it, withering and declining in its wake.

As a species that seeks to extend its existence, we must make the most of the window of opportunity that we've been given to change public opinion. Such a change cannot be dictated from above. It needs to come from us through the influence of the environment on us.

We will also have to relate to other elements, such as biological evolution, since our genes also develop. Thus, we need to address the need which makes women want to advance and get out of the house and cultivate their own careers.

While it's indeed a big change in the role of women, compared to what we've been accustomed to seeing over the last several decades, if we don't restore the natural balance in the woman's role, we will regrettably witness humanity slipping into the abyss, and a generation that will continue to slide toward drugs, prostitution, and crime. The school system cannot replace the family.

The only thing that can mend today's disintegrating society is a woman who understands her significance in the equation. Therefore, we must all come together to change women's status. We must demand that women not be "toyed with" or "managed" because they are feminine, mothers and child-bearers. It is the woman who decides what will happen, how it will happen, and she determines the face of the world. Women have the intellect and sensitivity, the flexibility, and the level of development required to grasp changes quickly.

We must cultivate the importance of women's role in the family because without it, the next generation will not be able to or enjoy life. We can see what is happening in the world; each generation is more lost than its antecedent, more disoriented and aimless. We want the next generation to be a good, happy generation, and who is better qualified to carry out this task than women?

We must teach women sciences, psychology, education, and any other contemporary knowledge to give them a substantial role in building the new world's education system. That role will require that she takes courses in education, management of the modern family, knows what children are learning, and works alongside the authorities. Women will have to be constantly updated on new programs and trainings to strengthen their inner core and their families' inner core, as well.

Everything depends on education and training, and if we seek to bring humanity to a human level, we will have no choice but to do it through women, through mothers. We will not be able to make anything of the next generation without education, without giving people values, content, and tools that will guard them through life. Only a mother can fulfill her children in that manner and equip them for life.

In the end, 90% of what men/husbands do stems from the influence of the wife. They aim to please her. Therefore, if we qualified women in the psychology of human relations, they would discover that they have all the tools to run the world.

But women have lost that important role; they lost their core, and the whole of humanity suffers as a result. It began in the 1960s, when women began to join the job market in great numbers. To provide for the needs of the modern family, women had no choice but to get a job, to help with the household income. There are those who consider this progress, but not all human developments are in our favor, as we can see in many areas in our lives.

There are many reasons why women went out of the home and into the job market. The American dream dominated our lives, and the idea that a family needs a house in the suburbs, two cars in the driveway, and gadgets and appliances galore, caused a rising tide of women to race out to find jobs. For the most part, women went to work because there was no other choice.

Humanity was supposed to advance from generation to generation in education, culture, and family relations. But are we really advancing in these areas? Is this development? As we can see, families are being ruined, children don't know their parents, and the parents don't know what their children need or how to give it to them. Thus, both parents and children are not brought up to live at home, or to be in a warm, close, and supportive environment.

We're missing out on the next generation. If we look at the statistics of crime rate, depression, and other illnesses in society, we will understand what we can avoid if families become families again. The crime rate will drop, and numerous domestic problems will be solved. The change will project warmth and gentleness throughout the whole of society, including men, women, and children. All this is possible, and depends on the importance we ascribe to it. In fact, we can do it here and now, instead of waiting for an even bigger crisis.

Women need to understand that they, too, need to align themselves with Nature because in the end, we all want to have a good life. We need to learn what the laws of Nature require of us, and see if we can align ourselves with these laws. This is the only way.

We must rely on scientists and psychologists who understand how the system of Nature's laws operates. We can rely on economists and statistical studies to present data on how we are being "brainwashed." We need to understand that public opinion experts create bogus fashions and trends, actually fooling us and compelling us to consume and buy excessively, and to adhere to certain views on life.

Only women can see how bad this situation is, and only a feminine force can change it. If they want to, women can do it. We should explain this to all the women's organizations and that, with their help, it's possible to change public opinion. Each organization will work in its own area to raise women's awareness about the family and to determine the woman's status as the center of the family and life.

When this awareness permeates the public view, women can demand regulations that will solidify their status. If women unite, it will be a huge force that no government can withstand. Women will be able to pass any law they want. Women's organizations will understand that the solution is simple: to bring out and extol the natural qualities of women.

To summarize, we should emphasize that women need to establish for themselves university courses, trainings, and various courses to acquire knowledge and excel in all areas of life, including education, culture, psychology, and economy. This should be done so they can complement their children's education, in addition to the ordinary teaching they receive at school, so that each child will be unique in his or her specialty. If we begin to correct the current negative situation in society, which is not in sync with the laws of Nature, and tend to it correctly, positively, inculcating public opinion with the proper explanations, we will have immense power at our disposal—the power of the feminine force, and the masculine force, as well.

CHAPTER FIFTEEN

Prisons as Education Centers

HOW INMATES CAN HELP SOCIETY

Many studies in criminology doubt the effectiveness of prison sentences as a means of crime prevention. The influence of prisons on inmates, especially with regard to deterrence and rehabilitation, is a topic that requires serious rethinking. Many countries are experiencing a rise in crime rate in both the number of incidents and their severity. Moreover, the data show that inmates who have been released from prison return to it on similar charges.

There are many causes for the rise in criminal activity, but the common denominator is the inability of our society to provide proper education. On the one hand, since they are very young, children are exposed to crime, violence, aggressive behavior, and competitiveness. On the other hand, the institutes charged with educating the children are neglecting values and wrongly focus on grades and tests.

But not only schools contribute to the problem. When our child comes home from school, we ask, "How was school? What did you learn? How did you do on the test?" In other words, grades are also the parents' prime concern.

At the same time, children are under constant social pressure at school. They have to cope with fierce competition, struggles over social status, envy, lust, violence, and drugs, phenomena we treat as "necessary evils." But are they really so?

Our schools aren't trying to turn youths into human beings, or educate them into being *humane*. We don't wish to see children as educational role models when they grow up, as good persons who know how to communicate with others properly, who know the difference between right and wrong, good and bad.

Spreading violence has become one of the biggest problems of society in general, and of schools in particular. It seems that schools have become hotbeds of future convicts.

Where have we gone wrong? Can it be that we are not raising children to be humane from the moment of birth? Is it possible that they are not being educated to resolve problems in the family, and do not receive tools and knowledge to educate their children in the future?

All too often we hear of children being abused by their parents. But the emotional abuse is all the more frequent, yet seldom reported. The logical conclusion would be that people were never taught how to be parents, or understand what kids are like and how they should be treated. Parents don't have good examples to give to their children.

The inclination of man's heart may be evil from his youth, as it is written in Genesis (8), but inclinations can be changed to good. They can be channeled toward avenues beneficial to society. For example, stubbornness can be turned into tenacity when striving to obtain a worthy goal, and aggressiveness can be turned into assertiveness when pursuing pro-social ideals.

In today's homes, children grow up watching violent movies and TV series, and play violent computer games. They are exposed to stories of violent crimes and sexual assaults. At school they are placed in a ruthless society that threatens their personal safety, where the more powerful are more successful, and in the end they are judged only by their grades.

What's more, good grades are not enough. You need to have better grades than your peers in order to be appreciated. This is how success is measured. Those who are born with natural talents use them against others, according to the examples they saw. The weak use their cunning and politeness. They are seemingly well behaved, but they are really not; they simply know their limits and have mastered the art of getting what they want, seemingly legally, but just as maliciously.

Children don't grow up in a vacuum. The patterns of our society and its rules are shaping these children, and the blame for how the children turn out is on the shoulders of society.

We are neglecting the most important thing in life— learning how to be good people in a good society. For example, we are not educating people about how to be good spouses, or how to maintain healthy family life, and indeed, families are falling apart. We're not teaching people how to relate to others, and we're not giving them the sense that they are part of an integral society where all are interdependent. A person who doesn't feel mutual dependence will act out of egoistic drives and do what is good for himself or herself, even if it's illegal, and even if he or she knows that a punishment awaits after the fact. Such people are dangerously uninhibited because they did not receive the right examples.

In our egoistic society, anyone can do what he or she wants, as long as it's not against the law, as long as the harm remains within the boundaries that society has set. But in an integral society, a completely different law is in power. A person must *give*, be integral, and aware of one's connections with all. Only when one keeps that condition can one be defined as "law- abiding."

The law is general participation, mutual guarantee, because everyone is everyone else's guarantors. This is why we need to show people how these laws operate. We see that Nature, ecology, and everything that happens in the integral, global world is pushing us to become partners. The fact that we are not receiving the proper education for it is the source of all our troubles.

Through education, we can prevent people from breaking the law. As part of the Integral Education, we can inculcate models of good connections that will be taught at school, and even at kindergarten. Instead of sitting in rows of desks in front of a teacher, children will sit in a circle, communicating with each other and learning to understand one another. We will experiment with rising above our egos in order to connect and build a group. This is similar to an elite unit or a sports team, where people have to unite and understand each other in order to succeed, thanks to their joint efforts and tight bonding.

We need to teach people how to be their own police officers. They'll know what they have to do, and it'll become a habit, second nature. Every unusual incident in class should be treated through a court-type discussion. In the discussion, the children will determine what was right and what was wrong in the incident, and will present all the arguments in the matter. In the scrutiny process, children will be moved and affected thus gaining impressions. Until children go through this process, they are not educated in the human sense of the word.

"Education," in the human sense of the word means that a child receives and experiences examples from life. The scrutinies will be done through discussions, court hearings, and role-playing. There will be a judge, an advocate, a prosecutor, and a jury. The entire process will be filmed, and the children will later watch the video and analyze their behaviors.

Everyone must partake in the discussion; children's roles should be changed and the scene re-enacted from different viewpoints. The re-enactment will show the children how opposite they can become from what they presented a few moments ago.

It's a very enriching activity, with children "absorbing" several roles and characters. This way, they learn to understand others even when the other's views are opposite. When a child experiences being both defendant and prosecutor, he or she grasps that there may well be another opinion completely opposite to his, but still valid.

As part of the Integral Education, children don't stay in school the whole time. They enjoy outings to places like banks, hospitals, factories, plants, and even prisons so they see how people work and what motivates them.

These outings should also be analyzed regarding the purpose of such visits. Through this process, children will learn that the whole world is connected, that everyone creates something for everyone else. In this way, they will broaden their horizons.

If we begin to rear children into human beings in this manner, and persist with education throughout their school years, we will move much closer to a good, balanced society, where people's personal safety will be restored. We will not fear sending our children to school or letting them out in the evening.

Today, the problem is that certain elements in society profit from violent films. But is this a good reason for us to let them corrupt our children? Children are the most impressionable beings, and we as parents have been charged with rearing them. As a parent, I don't let my son watch films or play violent games or be exposed to the bad examples we just described. I don't want him studying in a school that encourages arrogance and vile competitiveness, which lead to violence. I want to give him good examples. A person learns from the examples he or she sees, and we are not giving them good examples.

Therefore, to have a healthy society, we must make great efforts to change the existing education paradigms. If we speak to teachers and educators, psychologists, and sociologists, we will know what we need to do, and which limitations we should impose on society.

When we watch TV or surf the Internet, we experience many emotions related to violence, which shape our minds. Because we are aware of the negative effects these images have on our lives, and because we already have integral awareness common to many people throughout the world, we can stop the distribution of this type of content and ban their distribution through the media.

An integral society is one that thinks of the benefits to the people, unlike a democratic society that maintains that one can do anything he or she wants as long as it's not harmful and as long as the activity doesn't cause anarchy. One end of democracy is anarchy, and the other end is dictatorship. You need to choose where you are, decide what is the purpose of the different societies, and determine your own purpose. Democracy was meant to keep people's well-being in mind, but how is that to happen if we're all egoists? The benefit of the people must come first, before limiting the ego.

In many prisons in the world, not only are conditions disgraceful and degrade the inmates' dignity, but no real effort is done to rehabilitate them and make them good citizens. This is why punishments don't achieve their goal. Inmates who complete their term return to crime. They see it as a way of life. But if that's the case, why are people incarcerated? Should a person be jailed and just do one's time, or are we also obliged to turn that person into a corrected human being? What is the role of prisons?

In the remote past, there were countries in whom jailing was never implemented. The people there new it was useless. There were cities of refuge to which criminals fled, and it was forbidden to kill them there. But if a person was caught stealing, that person had to work in order to repay the theft. Each crime had its appropriate correcting punishment, but it was never incarceration. If we want to truly correct our situation, correction is not in material conditions, it's in education.

This is why prisons must become schools. Whenever inmates have free time, they must be educated. They must learn psychology, history, and what it means to be a human being. As part of the topic of becoming a human being, they will learn about the current, global world, which stresses the connections among everyone. And because prisoners are placed under the authority of the prison, they must be taken through an intensive educational program.

Today, prisons actually help prisoners become better professionals at committing crime! Prisoners meet experienced criminals and learn from them how to improve their skills. Naturally, this doesn't correct anything, but only adds to the corruption. Despite all the rehabilitating efforts by prisons, it is well known that only a few inmates reform themselves after their release, and create a life of normalcy. Most of them return to crime.

Human traits divide into two primary groups: internal, which we received by heredity and are in us from birth, and external, acquired through education, from the environment, the media, and society in general. Neither of these elements depends on the individual, even if they design one's personality and determine one's fate. Therefore, a prisoner cannot use them because the environment in which he or she is placed doesn't provide any good examples.

The rehabilitation framework must therefore change drastically. For examples, inmates can be divided into groups of 15-20 people and be led by a psychologist who will work with them and organize them. They will watch lectures on such topics as the structure of human society, the structure of the human being, human relations, human psychology, who we are according to our perception of reality and according to our behavior with one another, what is the ego that always governs us, and how we can look at ourselves from aside and criticize ourselves.

We need to turn every inmate into a good psychologist who understands him or herself, and can see the world from different angles. After such training, an inmate who comes out of prison can become a youth instructor because he or she has been through the negative path and has been reformed in prison. Once out of prison, such a person becomes an asset to society because of the ability to deeply sympathize with both ways of life. This makes a person a very positive and beneficial element in society.

As long as the inmate does not complete the correction process and becomes beneficial to society, it is best if he or she stays in prison and doesn't inflict further harm on society. Currently, we release prisoners from prison and basically await their return from that moment until they actually come back. So why have we wasted all those years? Why has society invested so much money and effort into that inmate? What has society gained? Who benefits from the inmate's time in jail if he or she didn't correct anything, and even returns to crime with greater efficiency after years in "crime school"—our prisons?

Therefore, courts that sentence people to time behind bars should become obsolete. Punishments shouldn't match the nature of the crime or its severity, but the time it will take to change the criminal into a positive element in society. Upon that inmate's release, he or she will be taught a profession and be sent to where the ex-convict can bring the greatest benefit to society. This is called, "the correction of society and the correction of man."

For example, there is no need to incarcerate a person who was caught stealing for the first time. Instead, that person can study at home or in a boarding school, and take exams that will testify to the completion of the training. Also, it makes no difference whether that person embezzled with customers' money in a bank, or is a pickpocket who stole something out of someone's purse. The criterion is determined according to the required correction process. As long as that felon has not been declared by society as corrected, he or she will remain in training. The idea is to provide people with effective correction, and these people will become the most positive and beneficial people to society.

The United States is a perfect example of failure in constructing a corrected society and balanced people. As a country, it lost its proper treatment of people a long time ago. In the current American society, a person cannot become a person of means through hard and honest work. The values in the country have radically changed, and while half a century ago modesty was a worthy trait, probably because of the dominant influence of religion, today what's valued is the opposite of modesty.

In classic capitalism, a person works hard and earns a decent living. That gives one pride in being a self-made person. But today, those who gain are those who can do "financial wizardry." These are the more respected and powerful people in society. This shift epitomizes the loss of the principles that used to symbolize America and the American spirit.

Citizens of the democratic United States possess more licensed firearms than any *army* in the world, including even the U.S. army. Altogether, there are about 300 million people in the U.S., and a similar number of licensed firearms in the country, one per every man, woman, and child.

The number of imprisoned individuals in the United States is also alarming. About one out of 100 residents of the U.S. is currently behind bars. This number is higher than even Iran and China, both relatively and in absolute numbers. And yet, crime is not letting up.

To effect change in this vast country, Integral Education must be implemented by law in all correction facilities. Inmates must be trained in both physical groups, as mentioned above, and through online courses, so that eventually they themselves will become educators.

A prisoner who trains to become an educator is no longer an ordinary person. It is a special individual, and this is how he or she should be trained. This is the condition for release.

In the time an inmate spends in jail, a convict must show that he or she can be among youths as a role model and educator. This is the purpose and this will be his or her profession upon release. It makes no difference whether that convict is a financier who stole billions, a beggar, or a bank robber. Everyone will come out of prison as educators because it's part of the rehabilitation process of the inmate.

The inmate will have to pass on to others what he or she learned as good examples. For example, graduates will join the staff of juvenile delinquency facilities, where they will have to show for the next six months whether or not they can educate the delinquents, change them, and set them straight. Naturally, their every action will be monitored and examined because it's their diploma, their ticket out of jail.

In jail, each inmate will take mandatory training in Integral Education. In fact, not just in jails, but everyone will go through this training. Without this training, it will be impossible to correct any of the crises we are currently experiencing in education, economy, or families. We are experiencing a psychological crisis and a crisis in health, with a startling increase in drug abuse, depression, and despair. Anything connected to people's personal or social lives is currently in a crisis. But as long as we fail to break the egoistic interests that profit from the global social crisis, we will not succeed.

Prisons can serve as great examples to the entire world. If we succeed in those places, we will also succeed in the seemingly "normal" society. Turning prisons into universities to construct human beings is nothing short of a revolution in social perception. The criteria for youths and adults, men and women are all the same. Whatever crime a person committed, he or she needs only to feel, understand, and regard oneself as an integral, and interdependent part of the environment. This is the foundation from which an inmate continues to grow.

The number of people behind bars in the United States points to the fact that American society is seriously ill. America cannot be proud of its democracy because democracy is meant to work *in favor* of the people. But having millions of people in jail proves that this democracy isn't servicing its people as it should. In fact, it shows that these people have been forgotten and are not being cared for. Behind the lip service about equal opportunities, American society is portraying disrespect for humans and for the education of the next generation of Americans.

In France, for example, there is culture, religion, family--all of which are foundations that keep people together. There is national pride in being French. It is a single nation, unlike America.

Because of the ethnic diversity in America, there is nothing tying them together. The deep disparity and lack of common language pose great difficulties and require an overhaul, a transformation of attitude, outlook on life, and values. And because Integral Education transcends all differences that create misunderstandings, it must be implemented in the United States.

Above all else, there needs to be an inclusive "umbrella" that says, "We belong to one nation, one country, one humanity, and one world. While keeping the uniqueness of each person, we must connect above it because Nature is compelling us." This is the right approach according to Nature's law. Nature is the one presenting us with our duty to connect beyond all differences in the integral world, in the integral society. We are connected whether we want to be or not. We have no choice; there is no other way to be saved from the troubles except by bonding.

If we begin to act this way in many places in the world, we will see how it affects the entire world. Today, it's difficult to influence fanatic and autocratic leaders, so the change depends on one thing only—someone who will step forward to serve as a role model. Only if that country first educates people will it demonstrate the necessity of Integral Education.

You cannot influence the world with your values and principles when your result is corrupt behavior. Therefore, if America wishes to set an example to the world, it must begin by reducing its number of inmates, by having more friendly and educated people, and by reducing the crime rate. When America is a role model in all those realms, it will be able to "export" its values to the rest of the world.

We have no intention of changing the law in America because this would be impossible. We want only to see that educators with expertise in social education be allowed into prisons. These people, skilled in working with people, will lead them into making the right, integral connection. They will organize classes inside the jails, and the inmates will be required to partake of them. Such studies could also take place via TV screens, the Internet, or by presenting the information on DVDs. Teachers would give lectures and conduct talks with the inmates, and psychologists would initiate activities. We should prepare educators for this approach now, and get permissions from prison administrations to turn prisons into schools for the education of inmates.

The achievements of the inmates will be announced in the media, and society will see what it needs in order to correct itself. In this way, we will learn that there is not such a big difference between those inside and those outside, because in regard to the laws of the world, of Nature, ecology, and human relations, we are all felons. All of us are to blame for what is happening in the world. There are no victims here; we're all equally responsible for the good and for the bad.

We are living in an integral world that is round, without beginning or end, so there is no one to blame. All the phenomena in human society are caused by everyone. We must achieve the nature of a uniform, integral society, and begin to relate differently to ourselves, to others, and to Nature, which created us, as well as everything else.

A New Engine for Life

For millennia, humanity has been asking itself, "Where are we headed? Where are we evolving? What should we change to improve our lives? And where is human nature leading us?" We've found ways to develop, but we were always drawn to the same direction.

After millennia of developing, we have reached a very interesting situation: The egoistic force that motivated us to develop has culminated, and has begun to decline. That force prompted us to raise our standard of living, learn more, understand more, and strive for happiness, wealth, and fame. But because of the decline in the thrust of the ego, a sense of fatigue and weariness has taken over to the point of depression and widespread despair.

We are living in the "now," and don't want to develop further or invest in the future. In fact, we're already changing, but we're going in the opposite direction to the process that has always driven us.

We are experiencing a comprehensive crisis that affects every aspect of our lives. This crisis is not unique to any one country or culture. It is a global crisis affecting every aspect of our lives.

It seems we have exhausted our energy and skills, of which we have a great deal. We've reached outer space and the depths of the oceans, but at the same time, we are depleting Earth of its resources. We can destroy life on Earth with the push of a button, yet we're still at the mercy of Mother Nature. But worst of all, we've lost our direction.

It's not as if the direction we were going was good, but at least it was pushing us to develop. Now, even that doesn't exist. We are beginning to wonder, "What's going on here?" "What's the meaning of life?"

The questions being asked these days concern us all, not just philosophers and thinkers. We've reached a point where we cannot develop anymore, but we also cannot remain at a standstill because by doing so, we will lose what development we've already achieved. The industry we've been developing for centuries is slowing down, science has reached a deadlock, and culture and social life have hit rock bottom, as seen on TV, which both drives and reflects our current values. Technically, we can do almost anything, but the content that fills our lives is growing lower, meaner, and superficial, in complete dissonance with our technological abilities.

Family life has rarely been worse than it is now. People feel alone, as though they are blind, searching their way from wall to wall inside a room. They are not meeting other people or knowing other people, and have no ability to connect with others in a proper, pleasant, and desirable manner. People are delaying marriages and the age of having children is rising. We're uncertain about our futures because our nature, the ego, this general evil that controls us, no longer aims us in any particular direction.

We're experiencing a profound crisis and great despair. Depression is the most common illness worldwide, the primary cause of many other ailments. We're in constant uncertainty about the present, and we fear the future, whether it's natural disasters or human-ego-made disasters, since we are totally out of control.

We know and understand all that, and many scientists have already recognized these trends. Even the majority of the public recognizes the above. Yet, other than diagnose the symptoms there is little we can do. We're helpless when it comes to solving this massive crisis.

We can think of this crisis as an illness affecting the whole of humanity. Its symptoms are dysfunction on several areas, like a body that's partially functional due to some imbalance in its systems. Likewise, the human society is not functioning properly; it is in disharmony and its systems are unbalanced. Yet, all we can do is recognize that we are governed by human egoism, ill will, envy, hatred, lust, and pursuit of power and respect. We're like a being that's about to destroy itself, along with the whole of civilization, but cannot stop itself. It's as if it knows the outcome of its conduct in advance, but is bent on suicide.

Due to the economic crisis, unemployment is on the rise. We have built industries that manufacture products that provide for needs that don't really exist, causing us to consume redundant products. Worse yet, to boost profits manufacturers make products that stop working much sooner than they should, just to keep us buying new ones.

Society cannot keep up with production, and when society slows down its consumption, manufacturers collapse along with the financial system, banks, insurance companies, and investment firms. Experts believe that in the foreseeable future, only ten percent of the world population will need to work in order to provide for our needs, while the rest of the people will be redundant. Hundreds of millions will thus be out of the job market for good.

The millions being ejected from the job market need to be occupied with a new, society-related occupation. They need to induce a social change, a transformation in human behavior, and bring humanity into balance with Nature. We need to engage in constructing a new human being suitable for the new era into which we are advancing. If the only problem we can see in the current situation is our egos, we can assume that as we change, we will rise to a higher degree than that of the ego.

This is how humanity has always evolved. After every crisis, a new situation emerged that seemed better, more just, and more advanced, and seemed to offer a new life. Subsequently, once we were established in the new structure, we found once more that not all was as we had hoped.

As we evolve, our development brings us states of suffering and negative situations. When the negative sensations and discernments reach a critical point, where we can no longer tolerate them, we revolt or declare war. Alternatively, we create change through our intellects via new perceptions and awareness. When this happens, new values and philosophies arise, allowing us to evolve into a new stage.

It seems that now we are faced with such a situation. We've already exhausted the previous situation, we see and understand that the cause of our plight is the ego, and we cannot continue letting it ruin our lives. Therefore, our nature demands change.

This is the uniqueness of our situation. We've never changed *human nature*, only switched to the next level of our development, like shifting gears in a car. We're already at the top gear, we've pressed the pedal to the metal, and the engine is losing power.

Now we have to change our fuel or change the engine. We have to change our course, our values, and our goals. The old engine won't work in the new area toward which we are "driving," so we'll need a new one. That is, we need to change human nature, the egoistic engine that until now has been pushing us to develop, discover, and perceive. The bottom line is that we *have* to change our nature.

There are two forces in Nature—the force of reception, our ego, and the force of bestowal, giving. These two forces create life. The combinations, balance, and harmony between them will make our lives better, more peaceful, and forward moving. We've come to a point where the force of reception, the ego, has stopped working, hence the sense of despair, which is sensed in every realm of life.

Scientists and researchers are beginning to perceive a solution: We need to change our fuel and adapt the engine to work on the force of bestowal, so the force of bestowal is in the lead, pushing us forward, with the force of reception being its subsidiary.

Human society has evolved. We have developed education, culture, industry, and especially commerce. In this way, we used the force of bestowal as a means to receive even more.

Now we are shifting to a new *modus operandi*, where the force of bestowal is the prominent factor, and the force of reception is but a means to an end. That is, we are moving into a new mode of work, new connections, and new relationships. We're changing the force in the lead.

We need to build this new engine so it works according to the force of bestowal. And since the engine is human society, we will have to deal with changing each person, as well as changing society as a whole. We needn't change industry or science, but the people who are involved in them and the relationships between us, and then all will be well.

To change ourselves, we first need a new way to educate people. The new education will see people as individuals and as a global group called "humanity." The questions that need to be asked regarding the new education are, "Who are we? What are we? How have we evolved over the millennia to our current state, and how should we evolve henceforth? What kind of change should we undergo, and by what means? How gradually should this change be implemented on each of us in person, and on all of us on the social, national, and international levels?" This change will affect all of human civilization.

Besides the learning, for which we also rely on studies of scientists, biologists, and sociologists, we need to develop the educational part: how we change and by what means. In other words, how do we arrive at a situation where the force of bestowal controls us and pushes us to advance instead of the force of reception? How do we realize these changes in people and society? How, and in which order, should changes be made with children, grownups, men, women, and in each society according to its mentality, religion, and tradition?

Today millions are being laid off from the "sweat shops" manufacturing worthless, redundant products. These people will shift into a new job—changing human society.

We will divide work reasonably among everyone, so we can all live in dignity, just as social animals do it in Nature. Among ants or bees, for instance, some are workers, some reproducers, and some are the food-makers. When we divide jobs among us similarly, we'll have to work only a few hours a day, perhaps not even every day. We will spend the rest of the time keeping human society good, proper, and in a state of well being. Here, all will receive what they need for dignified living. But the primary occupation will be self-transformation of each of us, and for all of us as a society.

Thus, we will form new education and a new society. The media will be filled with this new content, and the film and music industries, television, literature, and journals will be filled with stories concerning man's and society's transformation.

Today, this is our duty—to change humanity. This is why we initiated a series of books published by ARI Publishers, and are producing visual media content such as video clips and films for children and grownups. Our goal is to bring us closer to the changes we will all have to undergo.

About the Author

Professor of Ontology and Theory of Knowledge, Doctor of Philosophy, with a Master of Science degree in Medical Cybernetics, Dr. Laitman is the founder of the ARI Institute, with branches throughout North America, Central and South America, as well as Asia, Africa, and Western and Eastern Europe.

Dr. Laitman is dedicated to promoting positive changes in educational policies and practices through innovative ideas and solutions to the most pressing educational problems of our time. He has introduced a new approach to education, implementing the rules of an interdependent and integrated world.

A GUIDE TO LIVING IN A GLOBALIZED WORLD

Dr. Laitman provides specific guidelines for how to live in the new global village, our increasingly technologically interconnected world. His fresh perspective touches all areas of human life: social, economic, and environmental, with a particular emphasis on education. He outlines a new global education system based on universal values for creating a cohesive society in our emerging, more tightly interconnected reality.

In his meetings with Mrs. Irina Bokova, Director General of UNESCO, and with Dr. Asha-Rose Migiro, Deputy Secretary-General of the UN, he discussed current worldwide education problems and his vision for their solution. This crucial, global topic is in the midst of major transformation. Dr. Laitman stresses the urgency of taking advantage of newly available communication tools, while considering the unique aspirations of today's youth, and preparing them for life in a highly dynamic, global world.

In recent years Dr. Laitman has worked closely with many international institutions and has participated in several international events in Tokyo (with the Goi Peace Foundation), Arosa (Switzerland), and Düsseldorf (Germany), and with the International Forum of Cultures in Monterrey (Mexico). These events were organized with the support of UNESCO. In these global forums, he contributed to vital discussions concerning the world crisis, and outlined the steps required for creating positive change through an enhanced global awareness.

Dr. Michael Laitman has been featured in the following publications, among others: *Corriere della Sera*, the *Chicago Tribune*, the *Miami Herald*, *The Jerusalem Post*, and *The Globe* and on RAI TV and Bloomberg TV.

Dr. Laitman has spent his entire life exploring human nature and society, seeking answers to the meaning to life in our modern world. The combination of his academic background and extensive knowledge make him a sought-after world thinker and speaker. Dr. Laitman has written over 40 books that have been translated into 18 languages, all with the goal of helping individuals achieve harmony among them and with the environment around them.

Dr. Laitman's scientific approach allows people of all backgrounds, nationalities, and faiths to rise above their differences and unite around the global message of mutual responsibility and collaboration.

About the ARI Institute

OUR MISSION:

To promote a globally aware humanity for meeting the challenges of today's interdependent world.

WHAT WE DO:

- Encourage a dialogue between scientists, scholars and educators

- Promote positive changes in education policies and practices

- Create a new paradigm of integral education for all people

OVERVIEW:

Today's world is at a crossroads. There is worldwide evidence in the form of economic instability, political failure, and social unrest that humanity is going through a global change. As many experts are already seeing, the nature of that change is that we are becoming so interconnected and interdependent that the old systems are no longer working.

Since there is also ample evidence that the term "globalization" covers far more than the correlation between global financial markets, a more accurate meaning of the term should address the interconnected nature of society as a whole. We are "global" not just in the financial sense, but also, if not primarily, in the social sense.

The social unrest that began in 2011 and caught on like a global bushfire had demonstrated how social blazes can spread through continents, passing from one hot spot to the next via the wires of the World Wide Web.

We are all in one boat, and the sooner we all realize what is actually happening in the world, a safer and smoother transition will transpire.

While we have become globally interdependent, the mindset of self-centeredness still constitutes the predominant paradigm. Our interdependence has become a fact of life. But we, our way of thinking and our values, are still locked in the old paradigm. Therefore, the path to a viable solution for crises facing humanity today, must start at aligning ourselves with the new emerging conditions: we must educate and elevate ourselves to embrace our mutual dependence and responsibility for each other.

The problems that seem to tackle us around each corner are not the causes, but the symptoms of our real problem: lack of solidarity and mutual responsibility for one another.

Many researches have already shown the power of social influence. The ARI is working to harness the power of education and social influence to lift ourselves from the obsolete dog-eat-dog mindset, recognize the reality of an integrated human system, and adjust ourselves accordingly.

In today's globalized reality, either we all win or we all lose, because we are interdependent. When enough people in the world open their eyes to the facts of globalization and shared responsibility, a major shift will begin. No longer will countries and peoples exploit one another; no longer will mammoth consortiums exploit tens of millions of underpaid workers around the world; no longer will children be allowed to die of hunger and illnesses that can be treated with common antibiotics, and no longer will women be abused simply because they are women.

In a world where people realize that their own well-being depends on the well-being of others, they will care for others, who will later care for them in return. Terms such as "first world" and "third world" will cease to exist. There will be only one world and the people living in it.

Education means informing people of the new era of globalization, mutual dependence, and shared responsibility, of which we are all part. The recent global financial crises, and the series of uprisings around the world are sufficient evidence that we affect one another on all levels of life—economic, social, and even emotional.

The ARI is working to enhance unity and solidarity among individuals and nations, in congruence with the current, interconnected reality.

As we can learn from nature, unity, reciprocity, and mutual responsibility are prerequisites to life. No organism survives unless its cells operate in harmony. Likewise, no ecosystem thrives if one of its elements is removed.

Humanity is also an integral part of the natural system. Yet, we are the only species that, as a whole, still does not follow the natural law of mutual dependence and reciprocity. The ARI holds the notion that humanity is beginning to realize that we, too, are subject to interdependence and must play by that rule if we are to survive and prosper in the 21st century.

Embracing our interdependence, rather than ignoring or resisting it, is the key to our success in building a sustainable reality for ourselves and for our children.

Precisely because today's world is at a crossroads, the ARI is committed to a positive, optimistic view that we have a unique opportunity to achieve global transformation in a peaceful and pleasant manner. In light of all that, the ARI's mission is to promote a globally aware humanity for meeting the challenges of today's interdependent world.

Further Reading

The Psychology of the Integral Society

The Psychology of the Integral Society presents a revolutionary approach to education. In an interconnected and interdependent world, teaching children to compete with their peers is as "wise" as teaching one's left hand to outsmart the right hand. An integral society is one in which all the parts contribute to the well-being and success of society. Society, in turn, is responsible for the well-being and success of those within it, thus forming interdependence. In a globalized, integrated world, this is the only sensible and *sustainable* way to live.

In this book, a series of dialogs between professors Michael Laitman and Anatoly Ulianov sheds light on the principles of an eye-opening approach to education. Absence of competition, child rearing through the social environment, peer equality, rewarding the givers, and a dynamic makeup of group and instructors are only some of the new concepts introduced in this book. *The Psychology of the Integral Society* is a must-have for all who wish to become better parents, better teachers, and better persons in the integrated reality of the 21st century.

> "What's expressed in *The Psychology of the Integral Society* should get people thinking about other possibilities. In solving any difficult problem, all perspectives need to be explored. We spend so much time competing and trying to get a leg up that the concept of simply working together sounds groundbreaking in itself."

> --Peter Croatto, *ForeWord Magazine*

The Benefits of the New Economy:
Resolving the global economic crisis
through mutual guarantee

Have you ever wondered why, for all the efforts of the best economists in the world, the economic crisis refuses to wane? The answer to that question lies with us, all of us. The economy is a reflection of our relationships. Through natural development, the world has become an integrated global village where we are all interdependent.

Interdependence and "globalization" mean that what happens in one part of the world affects every other part of it. As a result, a solution to the global crisis must include the whole world, for if only one part of it is healed, other, still ailing parts, will make it ill again.

The Benefits of the New Economy was written out of concern for our common future. Its purpose is to improve our understanding of today's economic turmoil—its causes, how it can be solved, and its anticipated outcome. The road toward a new economy lies not in levying new taxes, printing money, or in any remedy from the past. Rather, the solution lies with a society where all support each other in mutual guarantee. This creates a social environment of care and consideration, and the understanding that we will rise or fall together, because we are all interdependent.

This book contains thirteen "standalone" essays written in 2011 by several economists and financiers from different disciplines. Each essay addresses a specific issue, and can be read as a separate unit. However, one theme connects them: the absence of mutual guarantee as the cause of our problems in the global-integral world.

You can read these essays in an order of your choice. We, the authors, believe that if you read at least several essays you will receive a more comprehensive view of the required transformation in order to resolve the global crisis and create a sustainable, prosperous economy.

A Guide to the New World:
Why mutual guarantee is the key to our recovery from the global crisis

Why does 1% of the world population own 40% of the wealth? Why are education systems throughout the world producing unhappy, poorly educated children? Why is there hunger? Why are food prices rising when there is more than enough food for everyone? Why are there still countries where human dignity and social justice are nonexistent? And when and how will these wrongs be made right?

In 2011, these questions touched the hearts of hundreds of millions the world over. The cry for social justice has become a demand around which all can unite. We all long for a society where we can feel safe, trust our neighbors, and guarantee the future of our children. In such a society, all will care for all, and mutual guarantee—where all are guarantors of each other's well-being—will thrive.

Despite all the challenges, we believe that change is possible and that we can find a way to implement it. Therefore, the book you are holding in your hands is a positive, *optimistic* one.

We now have a unique opportunity to achieve global transformation in a peaceful, pleasant manner, and *A Guide to the New World* tries to help us paqve the way toward that goal.

The book is divided into two parts, plus indices. Part One contains the concept of mutual guarantee. Part Two details the building of the new mutual guarantee society, and recaps the principles presented in Part One. The indices contain previous publications of the ARI Institute detailing its social, educational, and economic ideologies.

CONTACT INFORMATION

Inquiries and general information:
info@ariresearch.org

USA
2009 85th St., Suite 51
Brooklyn NY, USA -11214
Tel. +1-917-6284343

Canada
1057 Steeles Avenue West
Suite 532
Toronto, ON – M2R 3X1 Canada
Tel. +1 416 274 7287

Israel
112 Jabotinsky St.,
Petach Tikva, 49517 Israel
i.vinokur@ariresearch.org
Tel. +972-545606780